Make It a 5 Star Day!

Five Daily Acts That Change Everything

Make It a 5 Star Day!

Five Daily Acts That Change Everything

Kayla Hansen

Make It a 5 Star Day!
Copyright © 2017 by Kayla Hansen

First Printing, 2017

ISBN: 978-1541194892

Printed in the United States of America
CreateSpace.com

Buy copies of this book for your friends and family at Amazon.com or CreateSpace.com.
Kindle eBook also available through Amazon.

*Share your experiences in the Facebook Group: Make It a 5 Star Day!

✻ ✻ ✻ ✻ ✻

Special thanks to *all* my dear family and friends.
Particular thanks to my sisters, Janessa Orgill and Ashton Hosford,
for their insights on and passion for the 5 Star Day.
Above all, thanks be to God. He is so involved in our daily lives.

I'm also so grateful for all those who reviewed the book and helped
it become what it is. These individuals include:
Ashton Hosford, Janessa Orgill, Christine Hansen, Darci Page,
Robert Thiebaud, Nikki Hansen, Hannah Israelsen, Rachel Larson,
Cassie Adams, Carolyn Howe, Felicity Warren, Alex Withers,
Darlene and Dustin Sweeten, and Anna Skidmore.

✻ ✻ ✻ ✻ ✻

Table of Contents

Chapter 1

5 Star Day:

Super Valuable Background!

WHY HELLO, MY lovely friend! I am Kayla Hansen and I am thrilled to call you my friend. We are all brothers and sisters here on Earth. As children of God, our goal should be to follow the pathway that Jesus Christ has set. It is only through Him that we may once again live with our loving Heavenly Father in our heavenly home. Christ's pathway is the only place where we can feel true joy.

Like a great big team, we can strive to help one another in life's journey. We need each other! I believe that you are called to make significant contributions to this world and that you are irreplaceable and invaluable.

As I introduce this book, I want to recognize that every person on the earth is a unique individual with personal struggles and life circumstances. Despite our differences, we have a lot in common. There are similar threads of desire, worry, and need among all cultures and people. Amidst the challenges of life, do you want to be the best person you can be?

Thankfully, our earthly experience is not about becoming "the best" at everything, or even considered "the best" at anything. Rather, it is through the Atonement of Jesus Christ and His path of progression that, with time and diligence, we can become the best version of ourselves. Indeed, it is through this development that we can individually say, "I am becoming the *best me.*" This book can help us in this process of godly transformation.

Growing up, my family and I would listen to the words of the modern-day prophets and read the writings of the ancient prophets in the scriptures. The more I listened and read, my desire to learn gradually amplified. As I began applying the teachings I received, I found myself loving this endless treasure trove of divine help, doctrine, and knowledge. Yet in the process of this spiritual growth, I felt somewhat overwhelmed! With *so* many great truths and things to do, how was I to know what things I needed to apply on a daily basis in order to reach the goal of living with Heavenly Father? Is there a difference between *edifying* actions we need to be doing every so often and *critical* actions we need to be doing daily?

As I began college, more than ever before, my schedule began to be filled with many options I could choose to do each day. I often thought to myself, "At the end of the day, what are the essential actions that are pleasing in God's eyes and the most important for my spiritual well-being?" My sister, Janessa, confided in me that she had been wrestling with the same question. After a handful of inspiring religion classes, and prayerful study of Christ's life, she began to take note of things that were necessary for our daily spiritual welfare. Janessa organized her findings into five acts. She felt to call the days in which she accomplished these five daily acts a *5 Star Day*.

I liked this idea of having five daily actions to focus on. In the busyness of life I wanted to be sure I prioritized first things first, and I desired to confirm what five daily actions would lead to being founded on Christ's gospel and His path of eternal progression. With the five acts that Janessa utilized in mind, I began a journey that involved years of study and application of the holy scriptures and teachings of modern-day prophets. With time, I began to recognize patterns in God's teachings that constitute the things He asks us to do daily. These findings were not something new or out of the ordinary, and they helped me prioritize the most important things in a way that was fulfilling and easy to remember.

The results of these studies have changed my life and the lives of many others. Interestingly enough, the five acts that can allow for daily spiritual nourishment all begin with the letter S. I do not think it is a coincidence that the word "Savior" also begins with S.

There are a few differences between Janessa's original five acts and the five we will talk about in this book. Her original findings were wonderful, and the name she originally came up with deserves to stay. These five necessary actions truly do make for a *5 Star Day!*

As you read this book, you will find that I use a variety of real life stories and examples. And, I feel to say, you can expect a lot of my animated personality to shine through as well.

Now, I do not want anyone to think that the 5 Star Day comes from me or any mortal mind. I bear testimony that these five great habits for our day-to-day welfare come directly from the teachings of our Heavenly Father. I invite you to read each chapter of this book with an open heart and a willingness to "experiment upon [the] words."[1] It is an experiment worth testing. This is my sincere and simple invitation to you: *give it a try*, and *stick with it!*

The 5 Star Day should not be a passive and superficial check-list. These are sacred actions that should have a high priority in our everyday lives. When we sincerely choose to apply these 5 Stars, we allow for the teachings of the Savior to go from our "heads to our hearts."[2] I am experiencing this transformation process for myself.

Well, my friend (sigh and a crinkly smile), the time has come to introduce the 5 Stars! Here I will give you a brief introduction to

---

[1] Alma 32:27; John 7:17.
[2] Bonnie L. Oscarson, "Do I Believe?" *Ensign*, May 2016, 87; see also Mosiah 13:11; 2 Corinthians 3:3.

each Star. The 5 Star Day has everything to do with Jesus Christ and eternal progression. I have witnessed that consistent application of the 5 Star Day helps simplify *life* and sanctify *us*. The Lord is the great giver of peace and light.[3] We matter to Him; now let us reach up and show that He matters to us.

Make It a 5 Star Day!

✷ Scripture Study

Through personal experience and study of the Lord's words, I have learned that our relationship with the scriptures reflects our relationship with the Savior. The Lord longs to guide and bless us; His scriptures are "the key to spiritual protection."[4] Prophets throughout the ages have exhorted: "Remember to search [the scriptures] diligently, that ye may profit thereby."[5] The scriptures are essential for bringing the Holy Spirit into our day. "The sword of the Spirit, which is the word of God" is our weapon during our daily battles against the evils of this world.[6] God spoke of our day when He said "whoso treasureth up my word, shall not be deceived."[7] The Lord knows our hearts and personal circumstances, and He lovingly and willingly guides us. *Steadfastly hold to the word of God!*

✷ Sincere Prayer

You may think it is weird that this Star is not just the word "Prayer" (silly Kayla!). I promise the word "Sincere" is the most important part. We cannot have a full 5 Star Day without having true communion with our Heavenly Father. A modern-day apostle, Elder James E. Faust, taught:

---

[3] Isaiah 9:6; John 8:12.
[4] Boyd K. Packer, "The Key to Spiritual Protection," *Ensign*, Nov. 2013, 26.
[5] Mosiah 1:5-7.
[6] Ephesians 6:17.
[7] *Joseph Smith-Matthew* 1:37.

A fervent, sincere prayer is a two-way communication which will do much to bring His Spirit flowing like healing water to help with the trials, hardships, aches, and pains we all face. As we pray, we should think of Him as being close by, full of knowledge, understanding, love, and compassion, the essence of power, and as having great expectations of each of us.[8]

In our sincere prayers, we ought to plea for guidance to find someone we can help that day. This gives our prayers an action-filled meaning. As we do this, our days are filled with subtle yet significant miracles. "Counsel with the Lord in all thy doings, and he will direct thee for good."[9] *Sincerity is the key!*

✱ Service

The Service Star has everything to do with the daily "practicing" of discipleship and charity. The prophet, President Thomas S. Monson, said, "I know of no experience more sweet or feeling more precious than to heed a prompting only to discover that the Lord has answered another person's prayer through you."[10]

A potentially life-changing challenge was issued by the apostle, Elder M. Russell Ballard, in which he exhorted:

> In your morning prayer each new day, ask Heavenly Father to guide you to recognize an opportunity to serve one of His precious children. Then go throughout the day with your heart full of faith and love, looking for someone to help. Stay focused...if you do this, your spiritual sensitivities will be enlarged and you will discover opportunities to serve that you never before realized were possible.[11]

---

[8] James E. Faust, "A Personal Relationship with the Savior," *Ensign*, Nov. 1976, *lds.org*, The Church of Jesus Christ of Latter-day Saints, Nov. 1976 (accessed Oct. 20, 2016).
[9] Alma 37:37.
[10] Thomas S. Monson, "Peace, Be Still," *Ensign*, Nov. 2002, 53.
[11] M. Russell Ballard, "Be Anxiously Engaged," *Ensign*, Nov. 2012, 29.

5

Our families are the most important recipients of our best efforts and service. Each phase of life is distinct with this Star. "It is not requisite that a man run faster than he has strength," but we can ask ourselves, "What can I offer?"[12] We can do something for someone daily. It can be as simple as sending a loving text to a friend, sitting by someone sitting alone, making a lunch for your spouse, holding the door open, etc. The scriptures describe Christ as someone "who went about doing good."[13] We too can live in that remarkable way! I can confirm through personal experience the promise that "by small and simple things are great things brought to pass."[14] *Do something for someone every day!*

✳ S̲acred Time

Taking time to *reconnect with heaven* and *Remember* is the focus of the Sacred Time Star.[15] Sacred Time is interrelated yet distinct from scripture study and prayer. This Star can be different with each new day, and it should be customized to the individual. To help us with this divine need, there are certain holy places that are crucial in our lives. These places include: the church and temples.

These sacred places are unparalleled. The weekly act of going to church, and particularly partaking of the sacrament, brings renewal and helps us refocus on the most important things. Temples allow for peace and guidance and are the only places on Earth that have the Lord's divine authority to seal families together forever. Regular temple and church worship help us access the gift of Remembrance.

We cannot be at church or in the temple every day, so there are many personalized options that can help us reconnect with heaven and Remember throughout the week. For instance, stepping away

[12] Mosiah 4:27.
[13] Acts 10:38.
[14] Alma 37:6.
[15] 1 Chronicles 16:11-12; 1 Nephi 19:18; Mosiah 2:41; Mark 8:18; 1 Corinthians 11:2; Exodus 20:8-11; Isaiah 49:14-16.

from the busyness of life in order to play a few hymns on the piano may be a Sacred Time moment for one person. Going for a walk outside or taking time to draw a picture could be a Sacred Time moment for another. It is personalized to you. Seek for simple activities that help you "get away" for a moment with the objective to reconnect and Remember Christ's truths and His hand in your life.

Journal writing and family history work are so important, and they are potential Sacred Time moments. My mom, Christine, has taught the need to "turn off the noise" (cell phone, radio, social media) in order to have a Sacred Time moment of the day.

Being in holy places does not result in a Sacred Time moment without effort on our part. Choosing to reconnect with heaven and Remember allows for the promise that "[Christ's doctrine] shall distil upon thy soul as the dews from heaven."[16] Dew does not distill when there is constant wind. And thus it is in our own lives. "Be still and know that I am God."[17] *Reconnect and Remember.*

✱ Smile

I believe that smiling is a declaration of the heart. My sister, Janessa, has included the connection of gratitude with this Star. Gratitude and joy make up the foundation of the Smile Star. There is a reason the Lord exhorted: "Thou shalt thank the Lord thy God in all things."[18]

Joy and happiness are interrelated, yet they have significant differences. We can feel *Christ's joy* even at times when we may not feel *happy.*[19] The Lord encourages us to "cheerfully do all things that lie in our power."[20] President Thomas S. Monson taught:

---

[16] *Doctrine and Covenants* 121:45.
[17] *Doctrine and Covenants* 101:16; Psalms 46:10.
[18] *Doctrine and Covenants* 59:7&21.
[19] Russell M. Nelson, "Joy and Spiritual Survival," *Ensign*, Nov. 2016, 81-84.
[20] *Doctrine and Covenants* 123:17.

This is a wonderful time to be on earth. While there is much that is wrong in the world today, there are many things that are right and good. We can lift ourselves and others as well when we refuse to remain in the realm of negative thought and cultivate within our hearts an attitude of gratitude. If ingratitude be numbered among the serious sins, then gratitude takes its place among the noblest of virtues.[21]

Life is meant to be challenging at times. I know from personal experience that the Smile Star truly does brighten all the other Stars, and it illuminates Christ's light in our lives. *Be grateful and smile. Christ is joy.*

Make It a 5 Star Day!
* **S**cripture Study
* **S**incere Prayer
* **S**ervice
* **S**acred Time
* **S**mile

Many blessings can come from consistently living the 5 Star Day! There are times when I feel like there is something amiss in my life and I feel discontentment. Sometimes I feel off in my relationship with God and irritated with the people around me. When I begin to recognize these patterns, I analyze my day-to-day habits. I have come to find that I have been missing one (or several) of the 5 Stars in my day *every single time*. Over time, neglecting these daily actions in my life has inevitably led to confusion, unhappiness, and spiritual starvation. It truly changes everything! Consistency is important.

With diligence, tender care, and time, a seed is able to take root and grow—bringing forth its beauty and fruit.[22] I invite you to give

---

[21] Thomas S. Monson, "The Divine Gift of Gratitude," *Ensign*, Nov. 2010, 87-89.
[22] Alma 32; John 7:17.

8

the 5 Star Day time to *take root* and *grow* in your life. Stick with it! Remember, these Stars are not meant to complicate our lives. Rather, they are intended to simplify and enrich them! You are capable, and you are enough today.

Perhaps you have never applied any of these Stars to your life before or have gotten out of the habit. Come as you are. Perhaps you may need to start with just one of the Stars for now. If that is the case, I encourage you to start there and then diligently work your way to applying all five of the Stars on a regular basis.

The Lord taught that the two great commandments are: (1) love the Lord thy God with all thy heart, soul, mind, and strength, and (2) love thy neighbor as thyself.[23] Through experience, I know that life is more joyful, more purposeful, and full of light when we choose to diligently prioritize the 5 Star Day. These Stars are directly in line with these commandments to love God, love others, and love ourselves. This does not mean the storms of life will pass us by, or that we will not have complicated days, but we will have divine strength and perspective during those times. Our lives change continually, but Christ remains constant.[24]

I know that when we are having a quality 5 Star Day we can go to bed at night feeling peace, even if it was a hard day. I love you, and God loves you. We can do it.

Supplemental Stars! Booyah!

Here I would like to introduce you to what we will talk about in Chapter 9: *Supplemental Stars*. I have asked my friend to be the one to address you in that important chapter. These Stars are not among the foundational, irreplaceable Stars in the 5 Star Day, but they are extremely important. They have blessed my life in significant ways.

---

[23] Matthew 22:35-40; Mark 12:28-31; Jeffrey R. Holland, "The First Great Commandment," *Ensign*, Nov. 2012, 83-85.
[24] Moroni 8:18; Hebrews 13:8; "Be Still, My Soul," *Hymns*, no. 124.

The Stars in the 5 Star Day are like a sacred formula for nurturing our *spirits* every day. These Stars can be considered the "primary" or "fundamental" Stars. They are irreplaceable.

However, the overall well-being of an individual includes *physical* and *emotional health* as well. The Supplemental Stars can help us to function and thrive at even higher levels in all aspects of our lives. These Stars become even more crucial when battling emotional struggles:

Supplemental Stars
* **S**peak Truth
* **S**leep
* **S**weat (Exercise/Eat Well/Drink Water)
* **S**hower
* **S**upport
* **S**low Down
* **S**hine/**S**unshine

Again, these additional Stars can make a positive difference in our lives. Our bodies are gifts from Heavenly Father.[25] We can learn to love and make the time to care for our bodies as well as our spirits. It is a wise choice to incorporate the Supplemental Stars regularly along with the 5 Star Day.

How to Study This Book

My friend, I humbly promise you that there is much to be gained from reading this book and applying what you learn. So I am going to tell you how you can have the highest quality experience.

Some of the references you have seen at the bottom of the pages thus far may or may not be familiar to you. You will see references

---

[25] 1 Corinthians 3:16-17.

from the Holy Bible—which include the Old and New Testaments. You will also see references from the Book of Mormon—Another Testament of Jesus Christ. Other essential scriptural passages from the Pearl of Great Price and the Doctrine and Covenants are included. Talks and speeches by modern-day prophets and apostles are quoted often in this book. When a modern-day prophet or apostle is quoted you will often times see the title "Elder" or "President" before their names. I will define gospel terms that may or may not already be familiar to you.

Once again, the teachings in this book are not coming from me; rather, they are teachings from the Lord through His scriptures and prophets. If you would like to learn more about any teaching or topic, use the resources and references in the footnotes below as study tools. Any of the quotes, talks, or scripture references found in this book can be found at www.lds.org. If you want your own personal copy of the Book of Mormon or Bible, you can request free copies at www.mormon.org.

A modern-day apostle, Elder Russell M. Nelson, strongly emphasized, "Seeking to learn, understand, and recognize truth is a vital part of our mortal experience."[26] We learn in the scriptures that the Holy Ghost—or Holy Spirit—is the third member of the Godhead.[27] Among many sacred roles, the Holy Ghost comforts us, He provides us with personal guidance in our lives, He brings "all things to [our] remembrance," and He also helps us recognize what things are true and discern what things are not true.[28]

We also learn from the scriptures that the Holy Ghost speaks "in your mind and in your heart" by "a still small voice."[29] The Spirit is

---

[26] Russell M. Nelson, "Becoming True Millennials," Jan. 2016, *lds.org* (accessed March 2016); see John 18:37.

[27] 1 John 5:7; *Doctrine and Covenants* 20:28; *Doctrine and Covenants* 130:22; 3 Nephi 28:10-11; Matthew 28:19.

[28] John 14:26; John 16:13; Moroni 10:5; Ether 12:41; *Doctrine and Covenants* 39:6; 2 Nephi 32:5; *Doctrine and Covenants* 121:46.

[29] *Doctrine and Covenants* 8:2; 1 Kings 19:11-12.

felt rather than heard.[30] The feelings or "fruits" of the Spirit include: "joy, peace, faith," and "comfort."[31]

It is important to pay attention to and stay connected with our feelings. By practicing and learning how to recognize the Spirit's tender guidance, we will be able to sift through the negative, confusing, and deceptive voices of the world and know which voice is God's. What a miracle it is that through the Holy Spirit we have a sure way to identify eternal and unchanging truths. Our Heavenly Father has not left us to wander in the dark. God wants us to have guidance, and He wants us to experience joy! This experience becomes a reality as we strive to obey His commandments, follow His prophets, and sincerely strive to live a life patterned after our Savior, Jesus Christ.[32]

As we seek the Lord's eternal truths during our experiences here on Earth, there are many important questions we may ask. How can I feel close to God? Where did I come from, and why am I here? Where do I go when I die? How can I have more inner peace? How can I have divine help and guidance in raising my family? Does God still speak to His children now like He did in days of old? How can I be a better person? Does God know who I am, and does He even care what I do with my life? What should be my next step in life? All of these questions are valid. Having the faith and humility to ask such questions invites the Holy Spirit to begin to teach us. As we reach heavenward by study and faith, God will open up the windows of heaven. I encourage you to take the time to ponder and consider what a current question of *your* soul may be. It could be one of the questions just listed, or it could be a different question. Once you have gone through this self-discovery process, I invite you to read this book with a current question of your soul in mind (whatever it may be), and let the Holy Ghost teach you.

---

[30] Boyd K. Packer, "Reverence Invites Revelation," *Ensign*, Nov. 1991, 21.

[31] Galatians 5:22-23; John 14:26-27; Moroni 8:26.

[32] 2 Nephi 2:25; John 14:15; Doctrine and Covenants 21:1&4-7; 3 Nephi 27:27; Mosiah 2:41.

Coming up, we have <u>Chapter 2</u>: *Life's Purpose—An Essential Reminder* and <u>Chapter 3</u>: *The Great Miracle—The Gospel of Jesus Christ Restored in Our Day*. These chapters set the stage for understanding the "why" of the 5 Star Day. Highlighted in these two chapters are scriptural teachings about God's plan for His children, the incredible role of Jesus Christ in this plan, and the important pattern of God calling prophets. These foundational teachings have blessed my life, and I would be looking beyond the mark if I did not share them.

I highly encourage you to not only read these two chapters, but also to pay attention to how you feel as you read them. Please take the time to sincerely think about what is taught, and then prayerfully consider the truthfulness of these eternal concepts.

I invite you to study this book in a way that best fits your needs. You can study from start to finish or you can study by topic. Follow the Spirit in your studies and apply the teachings, feelings, and impressions you receive. Again, I love you, God loves you, and I know from experience that these things are true and invaluable. You are important to God.[33] May we reach up and show Him that He is important to us.

Well friend, let's take the Spirit as our guide, and let's get going!

---

[33] Matthew 6:28-30; 2 Nephi 26:24; Moses 1:6&12-13; John 3:16; Isaiah 63:7; Ephesians 3:19.

Chapter 2

Life's Purpose:

An Essential Reminder

BEFORE COMING TO Earth, we lived in heaven with God, who is our Heavenly Father. He loved and taught us there, and we are literally His "offspring" (His spirit children).[1] You and I—and every person who lives on the earth—are spiritually begotten of the King of Heaven, even our Almighty God.[2]

That can be hard to believe at times. Please read the references below, ponder them, pay attention to how you feel, and ask God in prayer if you are His child. I sincerely believe these things are true. The Lord's entire focus (His "work and glory") is the eternal welfare of His children.[3] President Boyd K. Packer taught:

> You are a child of God. He is the father of your spirit. Spiritually you are of noble birth, the offspring of the King of Heaven. Fix that truth in your mind and hold to it. However many generations in your mortal ancestry, no matter what race or people you represent, the pedigree of

---

[1] Acts 17:26-29; Romans 8:16; Hebrews 12:9.
[2] *Doctrine and Covenants* 76:24; Alma 30:44.
[3] Moses 1:39; 2 Nephi 26:24.

your spirit can be written on a single line. You are a child of God! [4]

God loves and knows us perfectly, and He wants us to become like Him.[5] Heavenly Father has a glorified and resurrected body.[6] If we had not received the opportunity to come to Earth and obtain physical bodies, we would have remained spirits. Likewise, without these earthly challenges and a body, we would have never been able to improve and progress from our premortal state.[7] The fullness of joy, glory, knowledge, eternal progression, and power that our Heavenly Father enjoys would be unobtainable without this testing period here on Earth.[8]

With the overarching desire for us to return to live with Him again—and experience godly growth along the way—our Father presented a plan. This plan is often called the "plan of salvation," or the "plan of happiness."[9] In order to fulfill our destiny, we would need to come to Earth, receive bodies, learn, grow, and be tested.[10] Christ is at the center of this plan. We will learn more about that in a moment.

The earth was created and all the beauties therein.[11] Adam and Eve were the first people to live; God created their bodies and placed into them their spirits.[12] Furthermore, the Lord placed them in the Garden of Eden where they lived in the presence of God.[13] They were in a state of innocence, unable to feel true joy because they could not experience sorrow or pain, and they did not know

---

[4] Boyd K. Packer, "To Young Women and Men," *Ensign*, May 1989, *lds.org*, The Church of Jesus Christ of Latter-day Saints, May 1989 (accessed July 9, 2016).
[5] Jeremiah 1:5; Matthew 5:48; 3 Nephi 12:48.
[6] *Doctrine and Covenants* 130:22; Luke 24:39; John 5:19.
[7] *Teachings of the Prophet Joseph Smith*, sel. Joseph Fielding Smith (Salt Lake City: Deseret Book Company, 1938), p. 181.
[8] *Doctrine and Covenants* 130:22; Abraham 3:25; Romans 8:17; Job 23:10; Acts 14:22; Revelation 2:10.
[9] Moses 6:62; Hebrews 5:9; 2 Nephi 9:6; Titus 1:2; Acts 10:10&12; Proverbs 3:13; Job 38:4-7.
[10] L. Tom Perry, "The Plan of Salvation," *Ensign*, Nov. 2006, 69-71.
[11] 1 Nephi 17:36; Genesis 1; 2 Nephi 2:14.
[12] Moses 3:5-7; Moses 2:26-30; Genesis 1:27-30; 1 Corinthians 15:44.
[13] Genesis 1-2; 2 Nephi 2.

what it was like to live away from the Lord's presence.[14] God gave them the commandments to multiply and replenish the earth (have children) and to not eat of the tree of knowledge of good and evil.[15]

Satan is an enemy to God, and with bad intentions he tempted Adam and Eve to partake of the fruit.[16] By eating the fruit of that tree, they *chose* to no longer remain in the presence of God, and their bodies became mortal—with the ability to die.[17] Also by eating the fruit, they *chose* to grow from their state of innocence, being able to experience sorrow and pain as well as joy and peace, and they would be able to have children.[18] By their *own choice* they entered into mortality; the Lord did not force them.[19] Neither did He force us. Adam and Eve began mankind's destined journey of this mortal experience, and the initiation of God's plan. Thank goodness! Now you and I could come to Earth and experience mortality.

Without the Savior, Adam and Eve—as well as each of us— would be doomed to fail. We would be in the power of Satan, with no ability to overcome sin and death; we would be forever cut off from the presence of our Heavenly Father.[20]

To help us on this journey, the Lord set forth specific guidelines called "commandments."[21] These sacred laws keep us on track and lead us home. They truly do not inhibit liberty; rather, we receive joy, divine freedom, blessings, and protection as we obey them. I have experienced these wonderful blessings in my own life.

When we follow God's commandments, we are proving to God and ourselves that we are willing to follow His path.[22] In significant ways, all the Stars in the 5 Star Day are directly correlated with the

---

14 2 Nephi 2:15-26; *Doctrine and Covenants* 29:39.
15 Genesis 1:28; Genesis 2:15-17; Moses 3:16-17.
16 Moses 4:6; *Doctrine and Covenants* 29:39; Genesis 3:1-7; 2 Nephi 2:17-19.
17 1 Corinthians 15:21-22; 2 Nephi 2; Genesis 1-3; Moses 4:22-25.
18 2 Nephi 2:22-25; Genesis 1:27-28.
19 D. Todd Christofferson, "Free Forever, to Act for Themselves," *Ensign*, Nov. 2014, 16-19.
20 2 Nephi 9:7-9; Mosiah 15:19; 2 Nephi 31:21; Acts 4:10-12.
21 *Doctrine and Covenants* 130:21; John 15:14; 1 John 5:2-4; Matthew 19:16-17; Alma 37:35.
22 Abraham 3:25; John 14:15; *Doctrine and Covenants* 130:21; 2 Nephi 31:10.

Lord's loving commandments. Applying these 5 Stars on a day-to-day basis helps us to come unto Christ and return home!

During our earthly experience, we are enticed by right and wrong. When we choose to do something wrong—or choose to do something against God's commandments or laws—this is called "sinning." When we sin we become "unclean" spiritually, and the scriptures teach that "no unclean thing can dwell with God."[23]

The thing is, due to our mortal weakness, we make poor choices every day. Because our faults would make us unclean before God, we would need someone to save us! Who could pay the price, and pave the way, for us to be "cleansed" from our sins?[24] This Person would have to be sinless and perfectly obedient to Heavenly Father, begotten of God in the flesh, and prepared for such a holy task.[25] Heavenly Father's love for us is so deep that He did indeed prepare and send Someone to rescue us from sin and death.

Through an excruciating sacrifice in behalf of *all* mankind, this Person would make it possible for us to "become holy, without spot."[26] Our eldest spirit brother, Jehovah—who is now known as Jesus Christ—accepted this sacred call to pay the price for *every individual*.[27] That includes you and I. Jesus would be the only Being to walk a sinless life on Earth, so if He did not provide the way for *us* to become clean, He would be alone in returning to live with God again. It was prophesied from the beginning of the world that our Savior would be born in the "meridian of time."[28] The meridian of time refers to the world's chronology being systematized with reference to the time of the Savior's birth (B.C. *before Christ* and A.D. *anno domini* i.e. in the year of the Lord).[29] The deep significance and impact of His mortal birth would be unlike any other.

---

[23] 1 Nephi 10:21; Romans 3:23; 2 Nephi 2:15-16; 1 Kings 8:46; 1 John 3:4.
[24] Isaiah 1:18; 1 John 1:7; 2 Nephi 25:23-26; Mosiah 4:10-13; Alma 5:21; Alma 7:14; Matthew 9:6.
[25] *Preach My Gospel: A Guide to Missionary Service*, 51-52; see Ephesians 1:3-4.
[26] Moroni 10:32-33; 1 Peter 1:19; John 3:16; *Doctrine and Covenants* 76:107.
[27] 2 Nephi 2:6-9; Abraham 3:27; 1 Peter 1:19-21; Isaiah 12:2; Ether 3:14; Ether 12:33-34; Colossians 1:15.
[28] Moses 6:57; Moses 5:57; *Doctrine and Covenants* 20:26.
[29] James E. Talmage, *Jesus the Christ*, (2006), 57-74.

Christ came to Earth with His message, ministry, and mission. After His saving truths had been taught (message) and His perfect example had been set (ministry), Christ did something that no one in the history of the earth had ever done—or could ever do save Him alone.[30] Jesus suffered and bled from every pore in the garden of Gethsemane where he offered Himself a ransom for our sins, underwent an excruciating death on the cross, and three days later rose from the dead (i.e. was resurrected). These three crucial events are collectively called *Jesus Christ's Atonement* (mission).[31]

Once again, Jesus Christ's Atonement includes the humbling truth that He suffered for our sins, died for us, and allowed for life after death. Two other aspects of His loving Atonement are worth mentioning. First, He willingly felt every pain, trial, hardship, and temptation that you and I—and every person on the earth—would ever experience.[32] Why did He do this? He did it so we would have someone who would know exactly what we are going through, and who would be able to console, send help, heal, and empathize.[33] He will be able to be our righteous judge because He understands us perfectly.[34] Second, His Atonement enables us to do things we cannot do on our own; this is called grace.[35] We never have to struggle alone.[36] Because of His Atonement, we can receive these unparalleled gifts:

- **Life after death, and ability to be clean from sin.**
- **Divine help in our trials.**
- **The capability to return to live with God and become like Him.[37]**

---

[30] Tad R. Callister, *The Infinite Atonement*, 5-8; see John 5:19.
[31] Leviticus 16:33; Alma 34:9; Romans 5:11; Isaiah 53:3-12; *Bible Dictionary*: Atonement.
[32] Alma 7:10-14; Hebrews 2:18; 2 Nephi 2:6-7; Psalms 147:3-5; Matthew 26:36-46; Mosiah 15:5.
[33] 1 Peter 2:24; Malachi 4:2; Mosiah 3:4-8; *Doctrine and Covenants* 19:16-19.
[34] Mosiah 3:10; Romans 2:16; 2 Timothy 4:8; 1 Samuel 16:7.
[35] David A. Bednar, "In the Strength of the Lord," *Ensign*, Nov. 2004, 76-78; see Jacob 4:6-7; Romans 5:21.
[36] John 14:18; *Doctrine and Covenants* 84:88; *Doctrine and Covenants* 18:10-13.
[37] Mosiah 3:13; Mosiah 3:19; Luke 22:39-44; 1 Nephi 11:32-33; Mark 16:1-6; Matthew 5:48.

It is our choice to apply the sacrifice of Christ in our lives or not. Without incorporation of this gift, we cannot make it home.

Satan—i.e. the devil or Lucifer—is also our spirit brother, and he revolted against God's plan.[38] Satan presented his own plan. He claimed that when we all came to the earth *he* would make sure that no one would fall short of returning home; he would force everyone to always make right decisions, and thus we would all remain clean to reenter God's presence.[39] Satan desired to take away our freedom of choice. As the finale of his plan, he demanded Heavenly Father's glory and honor for *himself*.[40] Satan would rob us of our agency and would stunt our ability to learn, apply Christ's Atonement, obtain a fullness of joy, and experience godly growth.

Heavenly Father spoke of the Savior's response to this scheme: "But, behold, my Beloved Son, which was my Beloved and Chosen from the beginning, said unto me—*Father, thy will be done, and the glory be thine forever.*"[41] Satan revolted against the Savior's divine calling.

Due to rebellion, Satan was cast out of God's presence. Of all of God's children, one third of them followed Satan and forsook the Lord.[42] "The heavens wept over [them]"; it was a very sad day.[43] Now he and his followers are here on Earth as miserable spirits that are unseen by our mortal eyes. Their objective is to tempt and lead astray those who chose God's plan.[44] Most of Satan's evil tactics correlate with his same burning desire to take away our agency (i.e. our gift of choice). Also—being that he does not have a body—he tempts us to degrade, hate, and mistreat our bodies.

Satan and his followers want us to be miserable like them. They desire for us to forsake God. They spread forth lies, temptations,

---

[38] Isaiah 14:12-15; Moses 4:1-4.
[39] Moses 4:1; Isaiah 14:12-17; *Doctrine and Covenants* 93:25.
[40] *Doctrine and Covenants* 76:25-31; Revelation 12:9.
[41] Moses 4:2; emphasis added.
[42] *Doctrine and Covenants* 29:36-37; Revelation 12:7-9; Abraham 3:24-28.
[43] *Doctrine and Covenants* 76:26; Luke 10:18; 2 Nephi 2:17-18.
[44] Moses 4:1-4, Isaiah 14:12-17; 2 Nephi 28:19-24; Genesis 3:13; 1 Nephi 15:24.

self-image distortions, and deception at every turn.[45] They want us to choose to hate ourselves and others, choose to doubt, choose to hurt, and especially choose to forget who we really are.

My brother-in-law, Josh, once made mention that an advantage had by Satan's followers is their knowledge about us from the premortal realm. They remember our life there, and they understand our divine potential. They know who Christ is and that His grace and truth are real. As for us, it is part of the validity of our test here on Earth that we cannot remember our premortal life, "for we walk by faith, not by sight."[46] We have complete advantage over Satan when we follow the Savior. Through Christ we conquer Satan.[47]

How do we sincerely follow the Savior and overcome Satan? How do we apply Christ's atoning sacrifice? How do we become clean from sin? What are the steps to return home?

"The Gospel of Jesus Christ"/The Steps to Return Home/ How We Apply Christ's Atonement

- **Faith in Jesus Christ.**
- **Repentance.**
- **Baptism/Taking the Sacrament weekly after baptism.**
- **Receiving the gift of the Holy Ghost.**
- **Enduring to the End.**[48]

These five essential commandments above are what the Lord calls His "gospel"; if we continually do these steps throughout our lives we will apply Christ's Atonement and live with God again.[49] Applying His Atonement in our lives requires effort, diligence, and

45 2 Nephi 2:27; 2 Nephi 28:20-23; James 4:7; Moroni 7:12; *Doctrine and Covenants* 10:5.
46 2 Corinthians 5:7; 1 Corinthians 13:12; *Doctrine and Covenants* 38:8; Ether 12:19.
47 *Doctrine and Covenants* 35:24; *Doctrine and Covenants* 10:5; Revelation 12:11.
48 Alma 7:14-16; 3 Nephi 11:31-38; Matthew 10:22; Acts 19:1-6; 2 Corinthians 7:9-10; John 3:5; Ephesians 2:8; Mark 13:13; 2 Nephi 31:5-21; Acts 2:38; 3 Nephi 19:5-15; 1 Corinthians 11:23-25; Alma 34:33.
49 Alma 7:14-16; John 7:16; 2 Nephi 31:3-21; Mark 1:14; 3 Nephi 27:19-29; 3 Nephi 11:31-38; John 3:5.

obedience. It is through this application that we can become clean, holy, and our best selves. Brad Wilcox, a religious scholar and inspirational speaker, gave this insightful comparison:

> Christ's arrangement with us is similar to a mom providing music lessons for her child. Mom pays the piano teacher. Because Mom pays the debt in full, she can turn to her child and ask for something. What is it? *Practice!* Does the child's practice repay Mom for paying the piano teacher? No. Practicing is how the child shows appreciation for Mom's incredible gift. It is how he takes advantage of the amazing opportunity Mom is giving him to live his life at a higher level. Mom's joy is found not in getting repaid but in seeing her gift used—seeing her child improve. And so she continues to call for *practice, practice, practice.*[50]

It is only fair that God asks for our faithfulness in order to fully access the matchless sacrifice His Son made for us.

Dwelling in God's presence is called eternal life, "which gift is the greatest of all the gifts of God."[51] It is important to remember that His doctrine is not complicated, life is.[52] We receive enhanced perspective with this thought from Brad Wilcox:

> He paid it all. It is finished. Right! Like I don't have to do anything? Oh, no, [we] have plenty to do...but it is not to pay that debt. [After our test is over] we will all be resurrected. We will all go back to God's presence to be judged. What is left to be determined by our obedience is how comfortable we plan to be in God's presence and how long we plan to stay there. The miracle of [His] Atonement is not just that we can be cleansed and consoled but that we can be transformed.[53]

---

[50] Brad Wilcox, "His Grace is Sufficient," July 2011, *speeches.byu.edu* (accessed May 4, 2013); emphasis added.
[51] *Doctrine and Covenants* 14:7; 2 Nephi 31:20; John 17:3; Romans 5:21; 2 Nephi 31:18.
[52] 3 Nephi 11:39; Alma 37:6; Matthew 11:28-30; 2 Nephi 31:3; John 16:33; Acts 14:22; Moroni 7:3.
[53] Brad Wilcox, "His Grace is Sufficient," July 2011, *speeches.byu.edu* (accessed July 20, 2016); see Revelation 20:12-13.

There is a pivotal preparatory time between death and our judgment day, and we are going to chat about that in the Smile Star chapter.

In terms of judgment day, the Lord declares, "For I, the Lord, will judge all men according to their works, according to the desire of their hearts."[54] We need not be afraid of judgment day if we are doing our best to follow the Savior. "In Hebrew, the basic word for Atonement is kaphar, a verb that means 'to cover' or 'to forgive'."[55] God promises that "if ye are prepared ye shall not fear"; if we have applied Christ's Atonement, it will both literally and symbolically "cover" our sins before the Lord—we will be clean before Him.[56] We will be assigned to a *kingdom of glory* for which our obedience has qualified us.[57]

To live with God again is to live in His presence in the kingdom called the *Celestial Kingdom (eternal life)*—this is the highest kingdom of glory, and a place of eternal progression and eternal families!!![58] When I speak of "returning home," this is the goal I am speaking of. This glorious kingdom is described as *"paradise"* and is likened unto the brightness of the *sun* in joy, glory, and progression; in comparison, the lesser kingdoms are reduced in glory and joy (Telestial Kingdom is compared to brightness of the stars, and Terrestrial Kingdom is compared to the moon).[59] It is only in the Celestial Kingdom that we can live with our families forever and that we can have a fullness of joy.[60] This is our focus! We were born to accomplish this mission. As we continually take the cleansing steps to return home, we can make it. We ought to live our lives in

---

[54] *Doctrine and Covenants* 137:7-9; Mosiah 16:10; Revelation 20:12.

[55] Russell M. Nelson, "The Atonement," *Ensign*, Nov. 1996, *lds.org* (accessed Nov. 7, 2016).

[56] *Doctrine and Covenants* 38:30; Hebrews 12:23; *Doctrine and Covenants* 76:69; Genesis 3:21.

[57] John 14:2; 2 Corinthians 12:2&4; 1 Corinthians 15:40-41; Dallin H. Oaks, "Apostasy and Restoration," *Ensign*, May 1995, *lds.org* (accessed July 19, 2016); *Doctrine and Covenants* 88:22.

[58] *Doctrine and Covenants* 76:51&69; *Doctrine and Covenants* 88:22; 1 Corinthians 15:40-42; *Doctrine and Covenants* 138:48; Moses 1:39; John 17:3; *Doctrine and Covenants* 14:7; Jacob 6:11; Hebrews 12:23.

[59] 2 Corinthians 12:2-4; John 14:2; *Doctrine and Covenants* 76:54-57; *Doctrine and Covenants* 137; 1 Corinthians 15:40-42; *Doctrine and Covenants* 76:71-80; *Doctrine and Covenants* 76:81-98.

[60] *Doctrine and Covenants* 93:26-33; *Doctrine and Covenants* 76:50-70; Psalms 16:11; Isaiah 51:11.

such a way that it will be a joyful reunion when we see the Lord again.[61] Our daily choices are preparing us.

May I boldly testify that the simple things in the 5 Star Day keep us "on track." Remember that "by small and simple things are great things brought to pass."[62] These five essential acts help us in taking the necessary steps to return home—especially as we endure to the end. Jesus Christ is the reason behind the 5 Star Day. Remember we are in the process of "practicing" the Lord's teachings through application.[63] Even if we have strayed from God in the past, we still have all the tools, ability, and right to accomplish our goal.[64] It is only when His Atonement makes up the "roots" of our testimony that no "wind or rain" can destroy our "tree"; only then "[we] cannot fall."[65] Christ must be our foundation, nothing and no one else will suffice.

Why are we talking about the plan of salvation? Because without the remembrance of the Lord's plan for our lives, why would the 5 Star Day even matter? If we were not in a daily battle against Satan, why would we need tools to protect ourselves? My friend, the battle is real. We are personally and as a family under attack every day! Satan is relentless in his efforts. The apostle Paul described this beautifully to the Ephesians:

> For we wrestle not against flesh and blood, but against principalities, against powers, against the rulers of the darkness of this world, against spiritual wickedness in high places. Wherefore take unto you the whole armour of God, that ye may be able to withstand in the evil day, and having done all, to stand.[66]

---

[61] Enos 1:27; Matthew 25:34; 2 Nephi 9:41; Helaman 14:29-31; Alma 5:15-19; Alma 5:38; Mosiah 15:28-29; Revelation 21:1-5.
[62] Alma 37:6; *Doctrine and Covenants* 123:16.
[63] Alma 12:24; Alma 34:32; Revelation 3:21; John 7:17; Isaiah 55:8-9.
[64] Matthew 20:1-16; *Doctrine and Covenants* 58:42-43; Isaiah 1:18; 3 Nephi 9:13-14.
[65] Helaman 5:12; 1 Corinthians 3:10-14; *Doctrine and Covenants* 50:44.
[66] Ephesians 6:12-13.

The 5 Star Day "protects" us and keeps us "practicing." The holy scriptures teach and remind us:

> Consider on the blessed and happy state of those that keep the commandments of God. For behold, they are blessed in all things, both temporal and spiritual; and if they hold out faithful to the end they are received into heaven, that thereby they may dwell with God in a state of never-ending happiness.[67]

I know these things are true. We matter to God, and I challenge you to put Him to the test. The 5 Star Day is rooted in the invitation to come unto Christ and use His atoning sacrifice to cleanse and transform us into beings fit to live once again in the presence of God. It is our destiny.

---

[67] Mosiah 2:41.

Chapter 3

The Great Miracle:

The Gospel of Jesus Christ Restored in Our Day

NOW THAT WE have jogged our memory of why we are here on Earth in the first place, there is another important teaching to remember before we jump into learning about the 5 Stars!

The Lord is the "same yesterday, today, and forever."[1] Isn't that wonderful? That means the Lord works in patterns! His patterns are a demonstration of His love for us, and His desire for us to have all the tools necessary to make it home.

From the very beginning of the earth, a recurring action of the Lord has been the call of prophets.[2]

The prophet is the Lord's "mouthpiece."[3] As His chosen leader, the prophet guides God's children here on Earth. If this relationship was likened unto a business, the Lord would be the "boss" and the prophet would be His hand-picked "executive assistant"—carrying out all duties under the direction of the boss for the benefit of the

---

[1] 1 Nephi 10:18; Hebrews 13:8; Alma 7:20.
[2] Amos 3:7; Hebrews 13:8; Ephesians 2:20; Numbers 12:6; Luke 1:70; 1 Nephi 22:2.
[3] *Doctrine and Covenants* 1:38; Amos 3:7; *Doctrine and Covenants* 21:4-5; Ephesians 4:10-15.

company. As God's mouth piece, a prophet has the sacred privilege of conversing with and testifying of Christ.[4] Prophets are yet another reflection of the Lord's love for us.

Now, any random Joe Goober in an alleyway can say, "I am the prophet called of God!" We are warned repeatedly in the scriptures to beware of false prophets.[5] The Lord will help us discern who has been chosen to be His mouthpiece. We are promised that "by their *fruits* ye shall know them" (i.e. by their acts, doctrine taught, etc.).[6]

In order to become the Lord's prophet there are two things that must take place: (1) the prophet must be literally called by God Himself, and (2) he must be given God's authority or permission to be His prophet.[7] This authority or permission is called the holy priesthood. The priesthood is the power and authority that God gives to man to act in all things necessary for the salvation of His children.[8] Only the prophet holds all the keys of the holy priesthood and the authority to lead the Savior's church—the prophet being under the direction of Christ Himself. In order to follow the Savior, we need to follow His chosen prophets.

Christ's prophets, and the people found within His church, are imperfect mortals that make mistakes. However, Christ's gospel found within His church is indeed perfect.[9] His atoning sacrifice is needed by all in the process of becoming pure and perfected.[10]

The Lord cannot be in charge of thousands of different churches with distinct beliefs. That would make Him an irresolute, changing, and indecisive God.[11] He loves all His children, even those who choose to be atheist. He loves us no matter what church

---

[4] Mosiah 3:13; Acts 10:43; Deuteronomy 34:10; 1 Nephi 22:2.
[5] Matthew 24:11&24; Helaman 13:26-29; Jeremiah 23:32; 3 Nephi 14:15; 1 John 4:1.
[6] Matthew 7:15-20, emphasis added; John 15:26-27; 2 Nephi 25:26; Mosiah 2:34-37.
[7] Hebrews 5:4; John 15:16; Matthew 16:19; Numbers 12:6; Exodus 33:11; Alma 13:1-16.
[8] "Priesthood Authority," *Handbook 2, Administering the Church.*
[9] David A. Bednar, "Converted Unto the Lord," *Ensign*, Nov. 2012, 106-109.
[10] John 14:6; Alma 1:26; Alma 6:5-6; Matthew 6:15; *Topical Guide to the Scriptures:* Perfect.
[11] 1 Nephi 10:18; *Doctrine and Covenants* 20:17; Hebrews 13:8; 1 Corinthians 1:3-15; Ephesians 4:5.

we are in.[12] However, it is important to observe—according to His patterns and order—that the Lord will only have one church that contains all truth.[13]

The Lord's church must have His laws, contain His name, and be governed by Him through His prophet that He has appointed.[14] When the fullness of His gospel is on the earth, God will always send forth missionaries to share these vital truths with the world![15]

When we receive words from His prophet, it is the same as if the Lord Himself is speaking.[16] What hope and comfort God's prophets bring! During Christ's mortal ministry, He taught:

"For had ye believed Moses, ye would have believed me: for he wrote of me. But if ye believe not his writings, how shall ye believe my words?"[17]

When we have a prophet and the Lord's priesthood on Earth, we have His sure guide. Let's name just a few of the blessings found on the earth when we have a prophet:

- Marvelous organization of Christ's church and the blessings found therein.
- Ability to fully access the Savior's Atonement with covenants and ordinances like: baptism, the sacrament, sealing families together forever in holy temples, etc.
- All resources to receive full forgiveness from sin.
- Capacity to receive the guidance and gift of the Holy Ghost.
- Authority given to preach and receive personal revelation in ordained callings and in our personal lives.
- Every tool necessary to know how to follow the Lord and navigate life's storms in the day and age in which we live.[18]

---

[12] Romans 8:38-39; John 14:15; 1 Nephi 11:17; Moses 7:28-33.
[13] Ephesians 4:5&11-14; *Doctrine and Covenants* 1:30; 1 Corinthians 1:10-13; Matthew 12:25.
[14] Amos 3:7; 3 Nephi 27:1-12; *Doctrine and Covenants* 115:4; *Bible Dictionary*: Church.
[15] Isaiah 52:7; Mark 16:15; Mormon 9:22; *Doctrine and Covenants* 18:13-17; Matthew 4:19; Matthew 24:14; John 21:17; Jacob 1:19; *Doctrine and Covenants* 42:6; Alma 18:39.
[16] *Doctrine and Covenants* 1:38; Amos 3:7; *Doctrine and Covenants* 21:4-5; Ephesians 4:10-15.
[17] John 5:46-47.

Remember that a prophet cannot be called without receiving the priesthood authority from God. Now, any random Joe Goober in an alleyway can also proclaim, "I have the priesthood of God!" Over generations, there must be an eventual direct-link to Jesus Christ in order for the priesthood to be considered valid.

When a prophet is called, how does he receive the priesthood? The priesthood is obtained by the placing of hands upon the head of him who is receiving it.[19] The person giving the priesthood must be someone who already holds it himself.[20]

Again, the priesthood is essential in order to call a prophet and to establish the Lord's church.[21] What is meant by "church"? The church is the "organized body of believers who have taken upon themselves the name of Christ by baptism and confirmation."[22]

From the beginning, God has organized His church here on the earth to give us all the tools to live with Him again. Remember those necessary steps we need to take in order to return home? We find those steps within Christ's church. That is why church is so important. Plus, the organization of His church helps us "practice" together as a team.[23] We need each other on this journey home.

The steps to return to our heavenly home only become valid thanks to the priesthood. Baptism, receiving the gift of the Holy Ghost, partaking of the sacrament, and all other saving ordinances are performed by the authority of the Lord's priesthood. Jesus Christ's church is governed by Him through His chosen priesthood holders.[24] He is a God of order.[25] And thank goodness for that!

---

[18] Gordon B. Hinckley, "We Thank Thee, O God, for a Prophet," *Ensign*, Sep. 1991, *lds.org*; Robert D. Hales, "Hear the Prophet's Voice and Obey," *Ensign*, May 1995, *lds.org* (both accessed May 1, 2016).

[19] Numbers 27:22-23; *Doctrine and Covenants* 107:40-50; Deuteronomy 34:9; 1 Timothy 4:14; Mosiah 18:18; Ether 12:10.

[20] Mark 3:13-14; *Doctrine and Covenants* 84:28; Acts 8:14-17; *Joseph Smith-History* 1:68-69; Haggai 1:13.

[21] *Doctrine and Covenants* 132:45; Ephesians 2:20; Ephesians 4:10-15; Alma 13:1-12; John 15:16.

[22] *Bible Dictionary:* Church; Acts 2:47; Mosiah 18:15-21; 1 Corinthians 1:10-13; 3 Nephi 27:1-12; *Doctrine and Covenants* 115:4; 1 Nephi 14:12&14.

[23] Alma 26:6; Acts 2:47; Moroni 6:3-5; Colossians 1:17-18; Romans 1:12.

[24] *Doctrine and Covenants* 50:26-27; Exodus 40:15; Luke 10:1; Acts 20:28; *Doctrine and Covenants* 107:25-26; *Doctrine and Covenants* 121:41-42; 1 Peter 2:9.

My sister, Janessa, once mentioned to me a parable that was shared by Elder Allan F. Packer. This parable relates the use of a passport to God's authority.[26] This can help us understand why it is so important to have the correct authority in order for the steps to return home to become valid. I will share this parable in my own words. Let's take our old pal, Joe Goober, as an example. Let's say Joe was living away from his homeland and tried to forge and create his own passport in order to re-enter his country of origin. Joe will not be permitted to enter. But why? It is his homeland! How rude of that country, right? Well, Joe's documents must be authentic with the proper credentials met in order to return home. This provides safety, clarity, and order. The Lord is the same way. Again, He is a God of order. The steps to return home—which include the covenants and ordinances that He requires—are the same for everyone. They are available to everyone, and we must go through His approved channel. This channel is His holy priesthood.

Wow, what phenomenal blessings we can enjoy when the Lord calls a prophet and the priesthood is on the earth! Unfortunately, we read in the scriptures a repeated pattern of the eventual rebellion of the people against the prophets.[27] Satan does not want us to have a sure guide; he does not want us to follow the Lord's servants.

When we follow the prophet we are blessed.[28] Once the people as a whole reject the holy prophets, the Lord removes His church, prophet, priesthood, and all the blessings we just talked about from the earth. This leaves us in a period of darkness without the Lord's mouth piece, and without His sure guide.[29] When this happens, it is called an "apostasy." This is not a happy period of time.

[25] *Doctrine and Covenants* 88:119; 1 Corinthians 14:40; 2 Nephi 6:2; Alma 13:1; Job 10:22.
[26] Allan F. Packer, "Spiritual Passport," *Family History, lds.org* (accessed Feb 3, 2016).
[27] Ether 11; Ether 7:23-26; Moses 8:16-20; Exodus 3:1-10; Jeremiah 26:8-9; Romans 11:3.
[28] Jeremiah 7:23; Alma 36:1; 2 Timothy 4:3-4; 1 Nephi 22:31.
[29] Abraham 1:2-5; Matthew 21:33-43; Mormon 8:7-11; 1 Nephi 1:20; 2 Chronicles 36:15-16.

Without God's authority and church on the earth, how are we supposed to take the necessary steps to return home? How do we *fully* access Christ's Atonement? The reality is, without a prophet and the priesthood we cannot fully partake of these blessings.

Thankfully we see another pattern in the scriptures. With time—because the Lord loves us—He has always reached forth His loving hand once again and has always restored His church, gospel, and priesthood by calling another prophet.[30] It is just a matter of time.

Please do not misunderstand or overlook this vital truth. So, for the last time, *every time* God has established His church on the earth—the means by which we can obtain all gospel truth and the steps to return home—the Lord has called a prophet. Every single time. This is an unalterable pattern of the Lord.

Adam, Enoch, Noah, Abraham, Moses, and Jeremiah are just a few examples of His holy prophets. We read of repeated periods of apostasy in between prophets. Consequently, the priesthood would be taken away from the earth. With time, a new prophet would be called with the priesthood given to him and the fullness of Christ's gospel would be restored.

Putting an end to yet another era of apostasy, Jesus Christ came to Earth and organized and directed the church Himself during His mortal ministry. When Jesus—the greatest prophet to ever live, even the Son of God—and His apostles were killed, the authority to speak God's words and lead Christ's church was yet again taken from the earth.[31] Once more, just like the periods of darkness in between prophets before, we were left in a state of spiritual obscurity without the priesthood and gospel.

This particular state of spiritual darkness or apostasy lasted much longer than times past. This time the people did not only reject the servants of the Lord but rejected the Savior Himself. This extended

---

[30] Acts 20:28-31; Isaiah 29:4&11-18; 2 Kings 17:13; Jeremiah 1:5&7; Jeremiah 7:25; Amos 3:7.
[31] Amos 8:11-12.

era of apostasy is known as the Great Apostasy.[32] Without another prophet called of God, we would all be doomed to remain in this abyss of confusion.

As a part of the turmoil and disorder during the Great Apostasy, changes were made to the Bible and many plain and precious truths were taken from it.[33] Thus there was a formation of many churches. Most of these religions had some parts of the gospel truth but not the fullness, and they did not have Christ's priesthood authority.

With time, there were many good people who recognized these unsolicited changes from Jesus Christ's doctrine, and they attempted to *reform* churches the best that they could. Martin Luther, John Calvin, and Huldrych Zwingli are but a few examples.

The "reformers" mentioned above were super important. They began the revolution of religious freedom which set the stage for today's great miracle. The fullness of Christ's gospel could now be *restored* through the Lord's calling of a new prophet and granting that prophet the priesthood. Again, this is God's unchanging pattern.

The Lord Himself taught through His ancient prophets that this Great Apostasy was going to take place after His death, but that one day He would call another prophet and there would be a "restitution of all things" (God would bring back what once was).[34]

My friend, I want to testify to you that the Lord followed His heavenly pattern, and has once again lifted us out of the period of spiritual darkness. He has called prophets and apostles once again in *our* day! I want you to read it slow, and read it one more time. The Lord has called a prophet in our day. Why wouldn't He?

Did God only speak to and guide His children in biblical times? Why would He only call prophets and apostles in days of old? Does

[32] "The Great Apostasy," *Doctrine and Covenants and Church History Seminary Teacher Manual*, 2013, Lesson 3; Acts 20:29-30; 2 Timothy 4:3-4; Galatian 1:6-8; 2 Nephi 27; Amos 8:11-12.
[33] Jeffrey R. Holland, "The Only True God and Jesus Christ Whom He Hath Sent," *Ensign*, Nov. 2007, 40-42; see also 1 Nephi 13:28-29; 2 Timothy 4:3-4; 2 Nephi 28:3-10.
[34] Acts 3:20-21; Amos 8:11-12; Ephesians 1:10; 2 Timothy 4:3-4; Isaiah 29:4&11-18; 2 Thessalonians 2:1-3; 2 Nephi 27.

God cease to be a God of miracles? The scriptures teach that He is no respecter of persons.[35] The worth of *every* soul is great in the sight of God—back then and now.[36] We matter to Him! These godly patterns have everything to do with you and I today.

Today's Great Miracle

During the age surrounding the year 1820, a young man—in Palmyra, New York—was consumed by the confusion of the times. With the loud voices of so many churches, this young man was being pulled in many different directions. The many religions contradicted each other in doctrine and worship. He described the struggle as follows: "In the midst of this war of words and tumult of opinions, I often said to myself: What is to be done? Who of all these parties are right; or, are they all wrong together? If any one of them be right, which is it, and how shall I know it?"[37]

Have you ever felt that way? The boy desired to know which of all the voices was correct and which organization was Christ's church. During this conflict, he read in the book of James in the Bible: "If any of you lack wisdom, let him ask of God, that giveth to all men liberally, and upbraideth not; and it shall be given him."[38] After he read this passage, he relayed:

> Never did any passage of scripture come with more power to the heart of man than this did at this time to mine. It seemed to enter with great force into every feeling of my heart. I reflected on it again and again, knowing that if any person needed wisdom from God, I did.[39]

---

[35] Acts 10:34-36.
[36] *Doctrine and Covenants* 18:10.
[37] *Joseph Smith-History* 1:10.
[38] James 1:5.
[39] *Joseph Smith-History* 1:12.

With time, this young man came to the conclusion that he must either "remain in darkness and confusion, or else...do as James directs, that is, ask of God."[40]

In the spring of 1820, this young man went to a grove of trees near his house. He knelt to pray, with the specific question in mind to know which of all the churches he should join. At this very moment, the young man related that "immediately I was seized upon by some power which entirely overcame me, and had such an astonishing influence over me as to bind my tongue so that I could not speak. Thick darkness gathered around me, and it seemed to me for a time as if I were doomed to sudden destruction."[41]

The boy exerted every ounce of strength he had to "call upon God to deliver [him] out of the power of this enemy which had seized upon [him]."[42] The young man recounted:

> Just at this moment of great alarm, I saw a pillar of light exactly over my head, above the brightness of the sun, which descended gradually until it fell upon me. It no sooner appeared than I found myself delivered from the enemy which held me bound. When the light rested upon me I saw two Personages, whose brightness and glory defy all description, standing above me in the air. One of them spake unto me, calling me by name and said, pointing to the other—*This is My Beloved Son. Hear Him!*[43]

Engulfed with amazement and light, this young man recognized these two separate heavenly beings as Jesus Christ and our Heavenly Father. The boy asked the Lord which of all the sects of religion he should join. The Lord answered that he "must join none of them, for they were all wrong."[44]

---

[40] *Joseph Smith-History* 1:13.
[41] *Joseph Smith-History* 1:15.
[42] *Joseph Smith-History* 1:16.
[43] *Joseph Smith-History* 1:16-17; emphasis added.
[44] *Joseph Smith-History* 1:19.

Face to face with the Lord, this young man—whose name was Joseph Smith—was the new prophet that the Lord called to restore the gospel of Jesus Christ to the earth.[45] This was not a reformation; rather, a *restoration*. Through God's chosen servant, Christ restored His gospel in full. I have learned for myself that the fullness of His gospel is found in The Church of Jesus Christ of Latter-day Saints. Christ is still the head of His church.

Due to the deep importance of what took place in this grove of trees, it has since received the name The Sacred Grove. This adds significance to <u>Chapter 7</u>: *Sacred Time Star.*

May I remind you that there is an unseen being with a host of individuals who do not want us to succeed? Think of the significance that Satan tried to stop Joseph Smith from praying. If this event was not vital for the eternal welfare of God's children, why would the adversary even care?

Satan constantly battles Christ's church.[46] Joseph later wrote: "It seems as though [the devil] was aware, at a very early period of my life, that I was destined to prove a disturber and an annoyer of his kingdom; else why should the powers of darkness combine against me?"[47] There will continue to be is a lot of opposition against The Church of Jesus Christ of Latter-day Saints. Satan is the reason why.

Joseph Smith received the priesthood from heavenly messengers who held it themselves—they having received it directly from Christ while they were on the earth.[48] Peter, James, John, and John the Baptist were these individuals. As another fulfillment of prophecies of old, Joseph received other keys of the priesthood for our day (i.e. this dispensation) from heavenly beings including Moses, Elias, and Elijah.[49] Like always, twelve apostles were called.[50]

---

[45] *Joseph Smith-History* 1:10-19; 2 Nephi 3:6-15.
[46] *Doctrine and Covenants* 10:5; Revelations 12:9; Moroni 7:12; James 4:7.
[47] *Joseph Smith-History* 1:20.
[48] *Joseph Smith-History* 1:66-75.
[49] Malachi 4:5-6; *Doctrine and Covenants* 110.
[50] *Doctrine and Covenants* 18:26-36; *Doctrine and Covenants* 107:23; Ephesians 2:2; 1 Nephi 11:34.

Additional evidence that Joseph Smith was called as the Lord's prophet was his translation of ancient American scripture written for our day.[51] It took him around three months (531 pages)! As a simple farm boy, he could have done this *only* by the power of God.

These writings were compiled and abridged by a prophet named Mormon, who lived in ancient American times. Being that Mormon was called to compile all the ancient records into one, the book is called The Book of Mormon—Another Testament of Jesus Christ. (This is how the members of The Church of Jesus Christ of Latter-day Saints received the nickname "Mormons").

During the Great Apostasy, God commanded Mormon's son, Moroni, to hide up the records until the time they would be brought forth by the Lord's prophet in the last days.[52] Centuries later, in 1827, Moroni (now an angel) showed Joseph where the records were buried.[53] By the hand of God, Joseph translated these records into the English language.

These sacred writings of the ancient American prophets take place at about the same time-frame as the Bible—two different places on the earth but the same God.[54] The Lord is aware of all His children in all parts of the world. The Book of Mormon is tangible evidence that the fullness of Christ's gospel has been restored today.

The crowning event recorded in the Book of Mormon is Christ's visitation to the ancient American people after His resurrection from the dead in Jerusalem. During Christ's mortal ministry, He taught the people in the Jerusalem areas: "Other sheep I have, which are not of this fold: them also I must bring, and they shall hear my voice; and there shall be one fold, and one shepherd."[55] Christ was speaking of the people in ancient America who had long-awaited

[51] "Book of Mormon Translation," *lds.org*; *Joseph Smith-History* 1:35-42&52; Exodus 28:30; Ether 4:5.
[52] Mormon 6:6; Mormon 8:1-4; Isaiah 29:9-18; *Doctrine and Covenants* 27:5; Ezekiel 37:15-19.
[53] *Joseph Smith-History* 1:30-33&59.
[54] 2 Corinthians 13:1; Ezekiel 37:15-19; 2 Nephi 29:7-11; 2 Nephi 3:11-12; 2 Nephi 27.
[55] John 10:16.

His visitation to them. [56] They were able to experience Christ's miraculous power and kindness and got to hear His doctrine from His own mouth just like the people in Jerusalem. [57] Jesus called twelve apostles in ancient America and gave them the priesthood to guide His church there.[58]

The Lord taught that "in the mouth of two or three witnesses shall every word be established"; the Book of Mormon is the Bible's second witness that Jesus is the Christ.[59]

Christ exhorted that we must be careful when we say, "A Bible, we have got a Bible, and we need no more Bible."[60] The Lord taught this vital lesson:

> Have ye obtained a Bible save it were by the Jews? Know ye not that there are more nations than one? Know ye not that I, the Lord your God, have created all men, and that I remember those who are upon the isles of the sea; and I bring forth my word unto the children of men, yea, even upon all the nations of the earth? Wherefore murmur ye, because that ye shall receive more of my word? Know ye not that the testimony of two nations is a witness unto you that I am God, that I remember one nation like unto another? [61]

We live in the "fullness of times," before the Second Coming of the Savior.[62] The writings of the prophets in the Book of Mormon and the Bible are for us in our day and age—the last days.[63] Both of these books are so important. Through my experiences studying the teachings in these two holy books, I know that the scriptures bring peace and guidance into our daily lives. In order to know if these

---

[56] 3 Nephi 15:21.
[57] 3 Nephi 11:6-17; 3 Nephi 11-30.
[58] 3 Nephi 12:1-2; 3 Nephi 18:36-39.
[59] 2 Corinthians 13:1; Matthew 18:16; *Doctrine and Covenants* 6:28; Ezekiel 37:15-19.
[60] 2 Nephi 29:6.
[61] 2 Nephi 29:6-8.
[62] Ephesians 1:10; *Doctrine and Covenants* 86:4; Moses 7:60-61.
[63] Mormon 8:35; 2 Nephi 33:10; Moroni 1:3-4; 2 Nephi 30:2-8; 2 Timothy 3:15-17.

books are indeed God's word, we must go directly to the source by prayerfully and diligently studying them.[64]

Again, the Book of Mormon is the Lord's tangible evidence that the restoration of His gospel has taken place. If that book is true, then Christ's true gospel and church have been restored. If that great book is true, then we have prophets and apostles today who are led by Christ Himself. *There is no gray area.* The last chapter of the Book of Mormon presents an important challenge and promise:

> Behold, I would exhort you that when ye shall read these things, if it be wisdom in God that ye should read them, that ye would remember how merciful the Lord hath been unto the children of men, from the creation of Adam even down until the time that ye shall receive these things, and ponder it in your hearts.
>
> And when ye shall receive these things, I would exhort you that ye would ask God, the Eternal Father, in the name of Christ, if these things are not true; and if ye shall ask with a sincere heart, with real intent, having faith in Christ, he will manifest the truth of it unto you, by the power of the Holy Ghost.[65]

I am a seeker of truth, thus I have taken this challenge that the Book of Mormon offers, and I know with all my heart that the Book of Mormon is indeed the word of God. When I read it I feel joy, guidance, strength, and I feel that God is aware of me. These feelings confirm to me that I am feeling the Holy Ghost and that what I am studying is indeed God's truth.[66]

Joseph Smith was killed at the hands of men poisoned by the lies of Satan. Joseph never denied what the Lord called him to do, and he never denied the truthfulness of the Book of Mormon. Would Joseph give his own life for a religion and a book that he just made

---

[64] 1 Nephi 15:8-11; John 7:17; Alma 34:4; 2 Nephi 28:30; *Doctrine and Covenants* 50:24.
[65] Moroni 10:3-5.
[66] Galatians 5:22-23.

up? A modern-day apostle confirms, "[He] would not do that!" [67] I have come to know for myself that he was called of God.

Since the days of Joseph Smith, the chain of prophets with the priesthood authority has not been broken and the heavens have remained open. Being that we live in the last days, we are promised that the Lord will not take His gospel off the earth again. [68] Thus, we have God's chosen prophet and apostles today! They guide and teach us how to come unto Christ now—just as in times of old. [69]

Why is it so important that we talk about the restoration of Christ's gospel in the 5 Star Day book? It is because it is SO vital to understand in order to comprehend the need for the 5 Star Day.

Why would we need to follow the current prophets—and apply the teachings of the Lord's prophets of old in the scriptures—if the restoration hadn't happened?

If you are someone who wants to know if God is real and/or has the desire to know if these things are true, the 5 Star Day will be of divine assistance in coming to know for yourself. You can come to know that this is indeed God's pattern and path for you to have joy, peace, and guidance. This has to be a quest undertaken with sincerity and with the intent to act upon the answers received. [70] And by golly it is worth it!!

If you are someone with the desire to deepen the relationship you already have with God, the 5 Star Day can magnify that desire in significant ways. You are capable and valuable.

I acknowledge that this chapter is bold, but it is not intended to be a sermon; it is intended to be a sincere invitation. No matter who you are, I invite you—with all my soul—to go to the true source by reading or rereading the Book of Mormon and asking God if these things are true. I likewise invite you to listen to any talk given by the

---

[67] Jeffrey R. Holland, "Safety For the Soul," *Ensign*, Nov. 2009, 88-90.
[68] *Joseph Smith-Matthew* 1:31; Daniel 2:44; *Doctrine and Covenants* 115:4.
[69] Ephesians 2:19-21; Ephesians 4:11-14; Ether 4:13-14, 18; 3 Nephi 27:19-21.
[70] Moroni 10:4.

modern-day prophet. Pay attention to how you feel—no matter how many times you have listened to the prophet speak. When we follow the prophet, we are stepping out of spiritual darkness and worldly confusion.[71] Lastly, I invite you to reach out to the missionaries of The Church of Jesus Christ of Latter-day Saints (in your city), and invite them to help you in your process of learning these things for yourself. These wonderful individuals are representatives of Jesus Christ, and they are called by the Lord to help you in your spiritual growth and application of these eternally vital truths.

The 5 Star Day has everything to do with Christ. Inevitably, every time we start making changes for the better, Satan will pitch a fit! It will not be as dramatic as Joseph Smith's experience, but he will surely try to deter us in any way he can. Satan understands the eternal significance that spiritual habits have in bringing us joy and closer to Christ in all aspects of our lives.

Guaranteed, Satan does not want us to come to experience these truths for ourselves. So we need to be on our guard. Satan wants us to mistakenly think that we are not capable or worthy of spiritual light and knowledge. Satan especially wants us to believe that we would be happier without it. *That is NOT true!!* If you have ever had any of these thoughts at any time in your life, I want you to know that Satan lied to you. Christ's path is joy! You are enough today!!

I promise that if you do these things with honesty and diligence, you will come unto Christ. With application of His atoning sacrifice, and diligence in following His prophets, you have power over Satan. Through personal experience, I know this is true.

With those important introductory chapters behind us, let's get going! Let's get learning about five habits that change everything!

---

[71] 2 Nephi 30:6.

Chapter 4

5 Star Day:

Scripture Study

WHEN I WAS a young gosling, I could often be found with my nose in a variety of children's books. I shared adventures with good old *Amelia Bedelia*, *The Magic Tree House* series, *Junie B. Jones*, you name it. I thought my books were pretty stinkin' neat.

One day, I saw the scriptures on my parents' night stand. It was tempting to keep reading my other books, but I decided to crack the scriptures open. I laid flat on my back on my parents' bed, and I lifted the Book of Mormon in the air above my face.

I do not remember where in the book I was studying, and I am pretty sure I could not even pronounce 50% of the words correctly. Nonetheless, I felt a feeling of joy while reading. The best way I can describe it is that I felt like a warm blanket had been wrapped around my spirit. For an extended amount of time, I stayed there reading and flipping through different sections of the scriptures. I felt tangible peace from the Holy Ghost testifying to me that the scriptures are of God and they are true.[1]

---

[1] Moroni 10:3-5; Galatians 5:22-23; John 14:26-27.

That experience is still engrained in my memory. From a tender age, I had experienced the reality that the scriptures are the words of the Lord and we can feel His love through them.

What exactly are the scriptures? A good way to think of it is that they are "expressed words, orally spoken or written by holy men of God that speak by the power of the Holy Ghost."[2] Thank goodness for the call of holy prophets so that we have these words! Ardeth G. Kapp describes the scriptures in a simple and beautiful way, "The holy scriptures are like letters from home telling us how we can draw near to our Father in Heaven. He tells us to come as we are. No one will be denied."[3]

Why is scripture study so essential that it is a Star in the 5 Star Day? The Lord teaches that the scriptures can be like "a lamp unto my feet," a source of truth that will "enlighten [my] mind," a guide allowing deepening of understanding to the point that my "mind doth begin to expand," and I can become "firm and steadfast in the faith."[4] We also learn the word of God "[heals] the wounded soul."[5] I believe we all have unseen wounds that can be treated as we read God's holy word. The apostle, Elder Bruce R. McConkie, testified:

> People who study the scriptures get a dimension to their life that nobody else gets and that can't be gained in any way except by studying the scriptures. There's an increase in faith and a desire to do what's right and a feeling of inspiration and understanding that comes to people who study the gospel.[6]

What hopeful promises from the Lord! Often times, life is full of unknowns, hazy mists, and even darkness. He did not send us to Earth without divine help.

---

[2] *Topical Guide to the Scriptures:* Scriptures.
[3] Ardeth G. Kapp, "The Holy Scriptures: Letters from Home," *Ensign,* Nov. 1985, *lds.org,* The Church of Jesus Christ of Latter-day Saints, Nov. 1985 (accessed June 20, 2016).
[4] Psalms 119:105; *Doctrine and Covenants* 11:13; Alma 32:34; Helaman 15:7-8.
[5] Jacob 2:8; "As I Search the Holy Scriptures," *Hymns,* 277. "Where Can I Turn for Peace?" *Hymns,* 129.
[6] Bruce R. McConkie, *Church News,* Jan. 1976, 4.

Press Forward, and Hold Fast!

In the Book of Mormon, a wonderful man and example to us all is the prophet Nephi. In case you are a history buff, Nephi and his family were guided by the Lord to the ancient American continent about 600 B.C. before their homeland, Jerusalem, was destroyed due to wickedness.[7]

One day during their travels, the prophet Lehi (Nephi's father) had a dream in which the Lord taught him many symbolic truths that apply to you and me. As Nephi pondered upon these important truths, he had a desire to see the things his father had seen. Nephi believed the Lord would make them known unto him, and He did.[8] In this prophetic vision, Lehi and Nephi saw many things. We are not going to talk about them all, but we will point out several key topics.

Among one of the first things Lehi saw in his dream was an exquisitely beautiful tree with white fruit. A modern-day apostle, Elder David A. Bednar, explained:

> The central feature in Lehi's dream is the tree of life—a representation of 'the love of God.' 'For God so loved the world, that he gave his only begotten Son, that whosoever believeth in him should not perish, but have everlasting life.' Thus, the birth, life, and atoning sacrifice of the Lord Jesus Christ are the greatest manifestations of God's love for His children.[9]

This tree representing the "love of God" was majestic and pure and it was next to the "fountain of living water."[10] As Lehi partook of the fruit, he learned that the fruit of this tree is "most desirable

---

[7] 2 Kings 24:10; Jeremiah 29; 1 Nephi 1:13.
[8] 1 Nephi 11:1.
[9] David A. Bednar, "Lehi's Dream: Holding Fast to the Rod," *Ensign*, Oct. 2011, 33-37; see 1 Nephi 11:21-22; John 3:16.
[10] 1 Nephi 11:8; 1 Nephi 11:25; 1 Nephi 8:10-11; Genesis 2:9; Luke 6:44.

above all things" and "most joyous to the soul."[11] The first thing he wanted to do was share it with others.[12]

So, for you and me, it is pretty clear that the tree is somewhere we want to be, and the fruit is something we should desire to taste. As we sincerely partake, the natural result will be a desire to share it with others. We need to get there and partake, but we also must stay true thereafter in order to live with Heavenly Father again.

As Lehi stood next to the tree, he saw in the distance that there were multitudes of people "pressing forward" towards the tree of life. Lucky for them, there is a "straight and narrow path" that leads directly to the tree.[13] Easy enough? Just stay on the path and you will make it to the tree! Well, I am sure it may take a little skippedy-loo and hop-scotch-skid-doo as well, but the path is straightforward and absolute, right? How hard could it be?

I have learned that everything in life that is *truly worth it* requires hard work. If important things did not require hard work, would they truly be worth it? That being said, what is the experience really going to be like in order to get to the tree of life? Here are some things that we will encounter on our way to the goal:

- The path leading to the tree is alongside a *filthy river* that represents "the depths of hell."[14] Wowzer.

- Across the river there is a "large and spacious building" that represents the "vain imaginations and the pride of the children of men."[15] It has *people pointing their fingers at us in an "attitude of mocking."*[16] They are loud and they are relentless. Super rude.

---

[11] 1 Nephi 11:22-23; 1 Nephi 8:12&15; Revelation 2:7.
[12] 1 Nephi 8:12.
[13] 1 Nephi 8:20-21.
[14] 1 Nephi 12:16; 1 Nephi 8:20-22.
[15] 1 Nephi 12:18.
[16] 1 Nephi 8:26-27; 1 Nephi 11:35-36; emphasis added.

- To top it all off, there is a *"mist of darkness"* representing the "temptations of the devil, which blindeth the eyes, and hardeneth the hearts of the children of men, and leadeth them away into broad roads, that they perish and are lost."[17] Good grief!

Okay, my friend. I need you to get in the zone, and truly imagine with me. The goal destination is the tree of life...you are far away from it...there is a mist of darkness blinding you to the point that you cannot see...you have a filthy river nearby threatening to drown you...and meanwhile there are a bunch of people pointing their fingers and mocking you as you strive to press forward. There is indeed *the* path that leads to the tree, but with the thick mist of darkness how do you even know if you are on the right path?

Wow. Thankfully Heavenly Father loves us so much that He has given us something that we can feel, something that we can hold on to. If we choose to steadfastly hold on and press forward, we will make it safely to the tree—our goal—and we will be changed along the way. This divine help is an "iron rod" that leads through the mists of darkness to the tree of life.[18] Imagine something like a firm banister leading you down the stairs to protect you from falling in the dark of night. Nephi taught his brothers about this safety line:

> And they said unto me: What meaneth the *rod of iron* which our father saw, that led to the tree? And I said unto them that it was the *word of God*; and whoso would hearken unto the word of God, and would hold fast unto it, they would never perish; neither could the temptations and the fiery darts of the adversary overpower them unto blindness...[and] destruction.[19]

---

[17] 1 Nephi 12:17; 1 Nephi 8:23; emphasis added.
[18] 1 Nephi 11:24-25; Revelation 19:15.
[19] 1 Nephi 15:23-24; emphasis added.

What is the iron rod? Ding Ding Ding! The scriptures! It does not say, "If you hold fast to the rod you PROBABLY won't perish and get led away by Satan." *The promise of the Lord is that if we hold fast to the iron rod, we will not perish nor be led away by the adversary.*

Semi-annually (in April and October), the modern-day prophets and apostles talk in a world-wide broadcast referred to as "General Conference."[20] The majority of the quotes in this book come from those phenomenal conferences. Remember that their words are just as much scripture as the words of ancient prophets. Their teachings are vital for our day. Hold on, and do not let go! Start today!

Ok wow. Lehi's dream is spot-on with the realities of the mortal journey we all face. If we want to live with Heavenly Father again, our relationship and consistency with the iron rod (the scriptures) is vital in our success. To reach our goal, holding to the iron rod is not optional—it is necessary and key. We literally cannot make it to the tree without it. We are taught that it is the word of God that leads us "in a strait and narrow course across that everlasting gulf of misery which is prepared to engulf the wicked."[21] The Scripture Study Star is a crucial part of how we keep practicing, and how we experience protection and transformation through the Atonement of Jesus Christ.

There were many individuals in the dream that hung on to the iron rod inconsistently, or only when it was convenient for them. These individuals are the ones the scriptures describe as "clinging" to the rod.[22] Sadly, these individuals arrived at the tree, and briefly tasted of the fruit, but "were ashamed, because of those that were scoffing at them; and they fell away into forbidden paths and were lost."[23] This is so sad. These people had the fruit in hand, but they

---

[20] General Conference Sessions, *lds.org/general-conference* (accessed July 5, 2016).
[21] Helaman 3:29; Helaman 15:7.
[22] David A. Bednar, "Lehi's Dream: Holding Fast to the Rod," *Ensign*, Oct. 2011, *lds.org*, The Church of Jesus Christ of Latter-day Saints, Oct. 2011 (accessed Nov. 20, 2016); see 1 Nephi 8:24.
[23] 1 Nephi 8:25&28.

left! They chose to believe the mocking voices, and distortions of Satan. My sister, Janessa, once pointed out to me that—in the end—they never found the "prize" they were looking for. They got lost in forbidden paths.

That is devastating! Thankfully, we can still get back on track. The Lord loves us so much that He will always send "angels" to help us discover, as well as rediscover, the tree. Alma the younger (Book of Mormon), and Paul (Bible), are two examples who experienced literal heavenly angels that were sent to help them get "back on track."[24] They chose to heed the Lord's call, and they never went back to their old ways.[25] This was still their choice. Nephi's brothers, Laman and Lemuel (Book of Mormon), also had an angel sent to them, but they repeatedly chose to reject the Lord's rescue calls.[26] Their choices affected generations of descendants.[27]

More often than not, the "angels" sent in our lives will be a friend, a coworker, a family member, a home/visiting teacher, the missionaries, a bishop, the list goes on. It is our choice to heed the Lord's rescue calls or not. May we learn from this part of the vision that we cannot just hold on to the rod when it is convenient, but we need to be steady and true. Starting today! You are never too far away from the tree to not get back on track.[28] Start simple, start now. Please come unto Christ. Satan lied to you when he told you that your choices do not affect other people and that the Savior's healing is only a myth.[29] The key is to steadily and diligently grasp that iron rod again. It is a promise from the Lord that the love of Christ will once again fill your soul.[30]

[24] Alma 36:6-27; Acts 22.
[25] Alma 4:20; 2 Timothy 4:7; Alma 48:17-18.
[26] 1 Nephi 3:28-31; *Doctrine and Covenants* 121:34-35.
[27] 1 Nephi 8:35; Jacob 7:24; 1 Nephi 15:2-3; Helaman 4:26; 2 Nephi 5:1-10.
[28] Mosiah 26:30; Jeffrey R. Holland, "The Laborers in the Vineyard," *Ensign*, May 2012, 33.
[29] Revelation 12:12; Helaman 5:12; *Doctrine and Covenants* 58:27-28.
[30] Alma 5:33-35; Jacob 2:8.

Elder C. Scott Grow taught, "[Your] foundation of faith can be diminished only through *neglect* or *sin*."[31] Pornography, immorality, drugs, violence, obsession with the virtual world, self-destructive thoughts and actions, and neglect of spiritual habits are *detrimental* to our spiritual safety.[32] We can harm our testimonies and spiritual growth through mistakes as well as apathy. Only through Christ can we start anew.[33] New beginnings are real. Hold to the rod today!

I have had different phases in my life in which my relationship with the iron rod varied in degrees of sincerity and diligence. I have felt the effects of the reality that my relationship with the scriptures reflects my relationship with the Savior. And my relationship with the Savior establishes my overall peace and contentment in life.

At a particular time in my life, I felt especially out of touch with heaven, did not feel satisfied about anything, and selfishly focused on myself. Upon reviewing my priorities, I noted my inconsistency and superficial attitude in terms of my daily scripture study.

In my mind's eye, I can see myself walking through the mists of darkness with the mocking lies of the world piercing my ears. I am walking alongside the iron rod with my fingers lightly touching it (here and there), but not really grasping on. What danger there is in that attitude! Remember, it is truly "by small and simple things" that "great things are brought to pass."[34] It is also by *neglect* of the small and simple things that Satan "leadeth [us] away carefully down to hell."[35] The river that represents the "depths of hell" is alongside the path—we need to be careful. Also, going to that great and spacious building will only lead to discontentment. With time, that symbolic building falls. Nephi saw "the fall thereof was exceedingly great."[36]

---

[31] C. Scott Grow, "Prophetic Principles of Faithfulness," *Ensign*, Jan 2017, 16-21; emphasis added.
[32] Linda S. Reeves, "Protection from Pornography—a Christ-Focused Home," *Ensign*, May 2014, 15-17; "Physical and Emotional Health," *For the Strength of Youth*, 25-27; see 1 Corinthians 6:19.
[33] Thomas S. Monson, "Keep the Commandments," *Ensign*, Nov. 2015, 83-85; "Repentance," *For the Strength of Youth*, 28-29.
[34] Alma 37:6.
[35] 2 Nephi 28:18-27.
[36] 1 Nephi 11:36; Job 4:8; Alma 41:10.

The Lord promises that those who "treasure up [His] word, shall not be deceived" in the last days.[37] Hold on to the word!

The meek, subtle heroes of Lehi's dream are those who held on to the iron rod with diligence and sincerity. These consistent people are described as "holding fast" to the rod.[38] In a significant way, these individuals humbly "came forth and fell down and partook of the fruit of the tree."[39] With the divine help of Christ's Atonement, this experience at the tree can be ours. It is meant to be ours.

When I find myself "holding fast" to the iron rod, or reading my scriptures with sincerity and diligence, my life is different. Life is not always easy, but I feel in touch with my purpose. I more easily see the good in others and the hand of God in my life.

We can feel peace and contentment during tough days. We are promised that when we are consistently "feast[ing] upon the words of Christ," rather than nibbling occasionally, we will be filled with the greater capacity to be a little kinder, more thoughtful, more spiritually-minded, more consistent with the most important things, and filled with the vision of the eternal potential in ourselves and others.[40] The scriptures give us power and guidance.

Get Our Amor On: Personally and As a Family

The Lord instructs us, time and time again, to teach our children the gospel.[41] We ought to be consistent in our personal scripture study so that we may more fully share eternal truths with our children.

When I was in elementary school, I decided it would be fun to teach one of my classmates a new board game (that I secretly did not know how to play myself). Yep, my logic was pretty awesome.

---

[37] *Joseph Smith-Matthew* 1:37.
[38] 1 Nephi 8:30.
[39] 1 Nephi 8:30.
[40] Gordon B. Hinckley, "Each a Better Person," *Ensign*, Nov. 2002, 99-100; see 2 Nephi 32:3.
[41] Mosiah 4:14-15; 2 Thessalonians 2:15; Moroni 8:10; 2 Timothy 3:15.

So, as we gathered the pieces together to play the game, my mind was racing with ideas of how I could make up my own directions. When it was time to start, I hesitantly proceeded to tell my classmate "how to play." As the game unraveled, I quickly discovered that there were holes in my instructions, and no real back-bone behind any of the "rules" I had made up. Clearly, the game ended up pretty lame. My poor classmate said, "Let's not play that one again."

That story makes me chuckle. Beneath the silliness, it teaches a valuable principle. We cannot truly teach something that we do not know ourselves. How am I supposed to teach others the gospel if I am not studying and applying it myself? Frankly, I cannot. I can try, but it will undoubtedly end up like my fake game. Not good.

From the Lord's modern-day prophets and apostles we are taught: "Whatever we must do to fit gospel study into our lives, the rewards will be well worth the effort. The light we allow into our own lives will reflect upon the lives of our children."[42]

Growing up, my family's scripture study was most consistent when we set a specific time of day to read, and tried our best to stick to it. We must be kind to ourselves and realize—with time—our small efforts make a lasting difference. We are teaching our children a pattern of bringing light into their lives. It is not always easy, but the Lord will help us as we just keep striving.

Perhaps you have heard the phrase "put on the [armor] of God." Well, when you think of armor what do you think of? Maybe you have flashbacks to *A Knight's Tale*, or Strider's flowing locks in *The Lord of the Rings*. Why do we use armor? We use it for protection in war. When we think of war, we may think of bombs, guns, jets, awful bloodshed, etc.

The Lord warned us of the daily combat that is not just physical, but spiritual and emotional in nature. Ephesians 6 teaches:

---

[42] "Family Scripture Study," *Ensign*, Oct. 1987; The Church of Jesus Christ of Latter-day Saints, Oct. 1987 (accessed August 2, 2016).

> Put on the whole armour of God, that ye may be able to stand against the wiles of the devil. For we wrestle not against flesh and blood, but against principalities, against powers, against the rulers of the darkness of this world, against spiritual wickedness in high places.[43]

This scripture is repeated more than once in this book for an important reason. We are in a war, my friend! Remember, the battle cry was made long before we even came to Earth. Our Savior, Jesus Christ, is called the "Lord of hosts" many times in the scriptures. He truly is the captain of the hosts of armies that fight for God.

We are to learn to discern between right and wrong, between truth and error. We are to choose whose team we are on. We already know that at the end of the war Christ will win.[44] If you consider yourself to be on the Lord's team, cheers to you! Now the question is: what kind of a teammate are you for Christ *right now*? You and I need to continually raise the bar, starting today. We are so valuable to Him.[45] Let's reach up and show Him that He is valuable to us.

Armor fortifies specific areas for maximum protection. With the armor of God, we learn it is necessary to have:

- "Loins girt about with *truth*" and our vital organs protected by the "breastplate of *righteousness*."[46]
- "Feet shod with the *preparation of the gospel of peace*" and our heads protected by the "helmet of *salvation*."[47]
- "The sword of *the Spirit*" (i.e. *the word of God).*[48]
- "Above all…the shield of *faith*, wherewith ye shall be able to quench all the fiery darts of the wicked."[49]

---

[43] Ephesians 6:11-12.
[44] Revelation 20:1-4; *Doctrine and Covenants* 29:11; Isaiah 11:6-9; John 16:33.
[45] 2 Nephi 26:24; *Doctrine and Covenants* 18:10.
[46] Ephesians 6:14; emphasis added.
[47] Ephesians 6:15, 17; emphasis added.
[48] Ephesians 6:17; emphasis added.
[49] Ephesians 6:16; emphasis added.

If we are not feasting upon the words of Christ daily, it is like running out to battle without our armor and without our sword (our tool to fight with). Yikes!

I have pondered a lot about the "breastplate of righteousness" that covers our vital organs, and I have studied the different designs of a breastplate. Some designs do not protect the back, and others do. It can be seen either way, but I like to think that we do *not* have something guarding our backs. In this case, we are not to run away from the enemy, we are to fight! My brother, Jake, noted that—if our backs are not sufficiently protected—this also gives us the greater need to surround ourselves with righteous influences. We are a team fighting side-by-side and back-to-back. Fight for our God!

To experience full protection, we need *all* parts of the armor of God: "Wherefore take unto you the whole armour of God, that ye may be able to withstand in the evil day, and having done all, to stand."[50]

Over the years, I have studied and applied many different ways to study the scriptures. These have included: reading during distinct hours of day, applying numerous study techniques, wearing various attires of clothing while studying, and even being in select places to study.

So what is the best way to study? There is no concrete answer to that. Scripture study experiences may be different as a child than as a teenager and as a young adult than as an elderly adult. The Lord is aware of our situations in life, and He will help us be able to fulfill our Scripture Study Star in an edifying way. The Lord will help us "get our armor on" according to our circumstances and desires.

Here are some ideas and teachings to help us better understand how we can improve our scripture study, no matter what our stage of life.

---

[50] Ephesians 6:13.

How Should I Study The Scriptures?

The overarching and fundamental guide to help us enhance and enjoy our scripture study is to do as Nephi did: "I did liken all scriptures unto [me], that it might be for [my] profit and learning."[51]

Starting our studies with a prayer is necessary in order to more fully apply what we read to our own lives. Prayer invites the Holy Ghost into our study, and He is the true teacher.[52] The scriptures become a guiding light when we choose to individually relate to the teachings, stories, and impressions we receive. We are to study in a way that best helps us come unto Christ. Remember the prophets' admonitions to "feast upon the words of Christ; for behold, the words of Christ will tell you all things what ye should do."[53]

Speaking of methods on how to feast upon the words of Christ, Elder David A. Bednar taught three helpful ways to study the holy scriptures. These divine strategies are interrelated and progressive in nature: (1) reading from *beginning to end*, (2) studying by *topic*, and (3) searching the scriptures for *connections, patterns, and themes*.[54]

Elder Bednar gave this promise, "Each of these approaches can help satisfy our spiritual thirst if we invite the companionship and assistance of the Holy Ghost as we read, study, and search."[55] For example, we could study a topic one day, continue our chronological reading another, and all the while keep our hearts open to patterns and connections. Mix it up and enjoy!

Using the topics that will be discussed during the upcoming Sunday lessons at church as our guide during the week can be helpful in outlining our studies. Taking notes, cross referencing, and marking verses are also helpful tools. Memorization of scriptural

---

[51] 1 Nephi 19:23.
[52] Dallin H. Oaks, "Teaching and Learning by the Spirit," *Ensign*, March 1997, *lds.org*, The Church of Jesus Christ of Latter-day Saints, March 1997 (accessed Jan. 20, 2017); see 2 Nephi 33:1.
[53] 2 Nephi 32:3.
[54] David A. Bednar, "Reservoir of Living Water," Feb. 2007, *speeches.byu.edu* (accessed Jan. 7, 2017).
[55] David A. Bednar, "Reservoir of Living Water," Feb. 2007, *speeches.byu.edu* (accessed Jan. 7, 2017).

verses that are impactful to you can be a powerful experience.[56] The use of a study journal can be instrumental in applying the scriptures to our own lives.

Each day after I have finished my study of the scriptures, I have found great strength and increased understanding by sharing what I have learned that day with someone else. Sometimes I may share my studies with one of my family members as we do a casual activity together, like washing the dishes. On another occasion, I may text a friend or share a simple post on Facebook with some gospel truths I was reminded of that day. As I study with the intent to share what I am learning with someone else, my studies are instantly amplified and it becomes easier for me to enjoy and relate to my studies. For some it may be helpful to read with another person until they feel comfortable studying on their own. Consistency is the key.

Christ was noted as being someone who knew the scriptures. He quoted them, and applied them to the distinct situations and needs of the people He was teaching. Knowing, loving, and daily gleaning from the scriptures blesses our own lives, and allows for us to be greater missionaries, friends, family members, and disciples of Jesus Christ.[57]

The amount of information, or how many chapters we get in, is not as important as the *sincerity, pondering,* and *application* of what we are studying.[58] Scripture study can be enjoyable and fulfilling.

For How Long Should I Read?

The prophet, President Howard W. Hunter, gave these great insights about effective scripture study:

---

[56] Devin G. Durrant, "My Heart Pondereth Them Continually," *Ensign*, Nov. 2015, 112-114; Richard G. Scott, "The Power of Scripture," *Ensign*, Nov. 2011, 6-8; see 2 Nephi 4:15.
[57] Alma 17:2-3; 2 Timothy 3:15; Psalms 19:7.
[58] John 7:17; *Doctrine and Covenants* 138:1-11; 1 Nephi 11:1; *Joseph Smith-History* 1:11-14.

It would be ideal if an hour could be spent each day; but if that much cannot be had, a half hour on a regular basis would result in substantial accomplishment. A quarter of an hour is little time, [however] it is surprising how much enlightenment and knowledge can be acquired in a subject so meaningful. The important thing is to allow nothing else to ever interfere with our study.[59]

My sister, Janessa, once took a religion class that had no homework other than the assignment to read the scriptures for *an hour* a day. She had an overwhelming busy schedule. She initially doubted her ability to be able to fulfill this assignment, but she trusted the Lord would give her strength. What first started as a daunting task was changed into a treasured hour of her day. She had all the energy she needed to accomplish everything in her busy schedule, and she recognized more fully the Lord's hand in her day-to-day life. Janessa has relayed that her decision to live up to this challenge changed her semester completely, and continues to have an impact on her life. She tells me often, "Kayla, life is happier and our schedules just work out when we prioritize our scripture study first." She knows from experience.

President Hunter refers to being able to read for an hour a day as ideal. I encourage each of us to take a look at our current life situations, and raise the bar a little by striving to live the "ideal" experience appropriately over time. Step by step.

Reading for *thirty minutes* a day changed the life of a young man named Andy Jorgensen. In the *Ensign* magazine, he shared an experience he had during a specifically trying time in his life:

I changed a portion of my day—just half an hour—and it changed my entire life. I found that President Benson was right; there is something more to the Book of Mormon. I

---

[59] Howard W. Hunter, "Reading the Scriptures," *Ensign*, Nov. 1979, *lds.org*, The Church of Jesus Christ of Latter-day Saints, Nov. 1979 (accessed Feb. 20, 2016).

woke in the morning and cheerfully greeted my Heavenly Father in prayer and my family at the breakfast table. I walked the same halls where I had before walked alone. No new friends appeared at my side all of a sudden, but thanks to [scripture] study, I felt companionship. The presence of ancient prophets and heroes and the Son of God that I had felt...stayed with me. The Holy Ghost was with me. I [lived] life in greater abundance. I was happy.[60]

Elder Gary E. Stevenson helps us realize how significant and simple it can be to read for even just *ten minutes* per day:

I recently learned that many...people spend an average of seven hours a day looking at TV, computer, and smartphone screens. With this in mind, would you make a small change? Will you replace some of that daily screen time—particularly that devoted to social media, the internet, gaming, or television—with reading the Book of Mormon? If the studies I referred to are accurate, you could easily find time for daily study of [that holy book] even if for only 10 minutes a day. Either on your device or in book form...I see you discovering answers, feeling guidance, and gaining your own testimony of [the scriptures] and a testimony of Jesus Christ. As you look to the book, you look to the Lord.[61]

My sister, Ashton, learned the *Five or Five Rule* as a significant guide for our very bottom line. If anything, we can read *five verses* or for *five minutes* every day. May we not let our heads hit the pillow at night without having read at least five verses or for five minutes. It is oh so doable, and so very important!

As we strive to have consistency, we can thrive within our given circumstances. Satan will try all his tricks and distractions to get us

[60] Andy Jorgensen, "I Changed My Life in Just 30 Minutes a Day," *Ensign*, July 2009, *lds.org*, The Church of Jesus Christ of Latter-day Saints, July 2009 (accessed June 1, 2016).
[61] Gary E. Stevenson, "Look to the Book, Look to the Lord," *Ensign*, Nov. 2016, 44-47.

to prioritize less important things first. He wants us to choose to neglect the armor that protects us from his lies. Satan has no power over us when we choose to follow Christ's path daily. Get that Scripture Study Star in! It is that important. Start somewhere!

What Time of Day Should I Study?

President Hunter continued his teachings about scripture study as he taught, "Perhaps what is more important than the hour of the day is that a regular time be set aside for study."[62] He also said, "When you have worries and challenges, face them by turning to the scriptures and the prophets."[63]

I used to read the scriptures *at night* most of my growing up years. It was a great way to end the day before going to bed. Even though sometimes I was tired, reading at night was good. It was very fulfilling for me at that time in my life. Two thumbs up for studying at night.

It was a hard decision for me to choose to switch to studying in *the morning*, but I had been given many promises that I would feel a distinct power during the day if I chose to make the switch. I made the change about the same time that I began working as a full-time nurse. Routinely, I woke up during the very early morning hours. Reading before going to the hospital required a lot of persistence, and my motivation increased as I felt an enhancement of the Spirit during the day. Throughout my shift, I would think of the things I read about. It gave me perspective and strength.

In my nursing career, there have been many times that the Spirit has guided me to double-check something or stop before giving a medication, and every time it was for the well-being of my patient. I contribute that divine help to early morning prayer followed by

---

[62] Howard W. Hunter, "Reading the Scriptures," *Ensign*, Nov. 1979, *lds.org*, The Church of Jesus Christ of Latter-day Saints, Nov. 1979 (accessed Feb. 18, 2016).
[63] Howard W. Hunter, "Fear Not, Little Flock," *1988–89 Devotional and Fireside Speeches*, 112.

scripture study. Perhaps you have had similar experiences in your own jobs and in your family. We truly need His divine help hour-by-hour, don't we?

I have known others who have set a fixed time *mid-day, after work,* or started the routine of a *split study session* (example: to study the New Testament in the morning and the Book of Mormon at night). Split study sessions can be quite effective as long as the times set aside to study are met. Whatever works for you, the most important thing is to be consistent. I promise consistency produces a positive difference in our lives. Some days are just nuts, but we are capable!

Where Should I Read?

We can read at a desk with our journal and pen, or outdoors in the calm of nature. Another opportunity could be to read in the car while waiting for our kids to finish school or to end soccer practice. Additional possibilities may include reading at a kitchen counter in the early morning hours, or in a rocking chair before going to bed. We can read in between tasks at work, or even while spending time in the bathroom (a mother's only place of privacy sometimes). We can study while nursing our babies, or we can listen to conference talks while making dinner. I have experienced that conference talks and scriptures on audio can be a wonderful blessing.

There are better places to read than others. It is wise to take note of those extra sacred places and choose to incorporate that type of study as often as possible. Eliminating the distractions associated with social media and texting can also allow for the Spirit to flow more abundantly. Changing our cell phones to airplane mode while we are studying can be helpful. The Lord yearns to guide and teach us. Daily scripture study can change everything!

Nine Months That Changed Everything

Seminary is a religion class for high schoolers. At the beginning of the new school year, a group of seminary students were given a blank piece of paper and encouraged to write their feelings about the gospel, faith, religion, the Lord, and whatever they wanted to write about. The papers with their responses were then gathered up and put in a safe place. Following that task, the students were presented a challenge with a worthwhile promise.

For the next nine months they would read the scriptures every day in class. The challenge was to mark them, note them, and apply them to their individual lives. In addition, during the nine months, the students were challenged to do two things: (1) pray on their knees—out loud—every morning and night, and (2) read a chapter of scripture each day on their own. The students were promised that if they took the challenge to heart, it would have an immense positive effect on all aspect of their lives.

And so it began, the nine month challenge with the potential to change their lives! Before they knew it, the nine months were up.

On the last day of class, the students were given another blank sheet of paper and instructed to write their feelings about God, the church, the gospel, faith, or anything they wanted to write about. Following this task, they were handed back the paper with their initial testimonies from nine months earlier. Many had forgotten all about it. They opened them up, and saw the change that had taken place in just nine months.

A girl opened her first response and—as she read—subtle tears began to roll down her cheeks. Her initial testimony and response from nine months earlier read:

> *I guess I sometimes wonder if Christ really does live. I don't know for sure, and I have always wondered since I was old enough to even think about it. . . . I also wonder if this is the*

true church or not. Everything we are told to do seems right, but I still have doubts.

After nine months of studying the scriptures, she wrote, in part:

I know God lives and His Son, Jesus Christ, is my Brother and He knows me and He cares about me. Through prayer I know He will guide us and show us the right way through His prophets, who I know are called of God. I know He loves each of us in a very special way. The Church of Jesus Christ of Latter-day Saints is the only true church, and I know it without a doubt. It was restored by Joseph Smith, who I know was a true prophet.

A young man opened up his initial paper, and shook his head in disbelief as he read his first response:

I don't really know there's a God. I only go to church to make my mom and dad happy. I wish I had a testimony, but I don't. Sometimes I feel like I have an important job on Earth, but I don't know what it is. I'm always wanting to do something wrong.

Nine months later this young man wrote:

I know the Church is true. I have a testimony of it. I love my Big Brother and my Heavenly Father, and I know They live. I know Joseph Smith was a prophet of God, and I have a testimony of it. I love this church with all my life. Some say they do not know if they would give their life for it, but I know—if need be, and my Father willed it—I would.[64]

---

[64] Todd B. Parker, "True Doctrine, Understood, Changes Attitudes and Behaviors," Jan. 2015, *speeches.byu.edu* (accessed Jan 7, 2017).

✹ ✹ ✹ ✹ ✹

I have a testimony that this transformation can come to anyone who is willing to seek God and truly make an effort. These students experienced President Ezra Taft Benson's promise:

> When individual[s] and families immerse themselves in the scriptures regularly and consistently…Testimonies will increase. Commitment will be strengthened. Families will be fortified. Personal revelation will flow.[65]

These seminary students had the opportunity to come closer to Christ as they diligently read and applied His word. *Steadfastly hold to the word of God!*

There are countless experiences that I could share about God guiding His children through scripture study. The experiences could be an entire book of their own. Here, I share just a few cases.

Helpful Examples

Example 1

As a young child I had beliefs that the scriptures contained the word of God, but it was not until later in life that I began to realize that the scriptures were the Lord's instructions *for me*.

I was a fun-loving, yet slightly shy, 14-year-old at my first experience at the summer youth camp called Especially for Youth (EFY). This wonderful camp is designed to help teenagers to gain a deeper commitment to live the gospel of Jesus Christ.[66] It is also a super fun experience with lots of wholesome activities. I went with my cousin, Melissa, and we had a blast while also choosing to grow spiritually. During this week-long experience, every morning we were given forty-five minutes to individually read the scriptures in

---

[65] Ezra T. Benson, "The Power of the Word," *Ensign*, May 1986, 81.
[66] "What is EFY? Especially For Youth," *efy.byu.edu* (accessed Dec. 20, 2016).

the crisp morning air. I had never read the scriptures for that amount of time in one sitting before. Despite that, I wanted to make the most of it.

Within ten minutes, I was increasingly interested in the scriptural passages. After thirty minutes, my soul was filled with light as I began making connections with these passages to my own personal life. Amazingly, I can still remember one of the verses that I read on the first day of camp.

I was in the midst of increasing moral turmoil at that time in my life. At school, I experienced the battle of being pulled in many directions by a variety of friend groups that had different moral standards. When I came across Alma 34:39 (Book of Mormon), it felt like a beam of light was penetrating my heart and mind. This passage of scripture reads:

> Yea, and I also exhort you [Kayla] that ye be watchful unto prayer continually, that ye may not be led away by the temptations of the devil, that he may not overpower you, that ye may not become his subjects at the last day; for behold, he rewardeth you no good thing.[67]

I felt an overwhelming feeling of God's love come over me, as well as a sense of warning. Being off of Christ's path would reward me "no good thing." I made a commitment to let go of the friend groups that were pulling me away from the pathway of the Savior, while still being kind to them. That choice changed my life's course.

That decision came due to a "hand written" note for me—from Heavenly Father—in the scriptures. *Steadfastly hold to the word of God!*

Example 2

As a young new college graduate, I had been working full-time as a Registered Nurse for many months. With time, the feelings of the

---

[67] Alma 34:39; word added.

Spirit guided me to know that I needed to make a change in my life, but I did not know what was meant by that.

I started praying for guidance to know if I should go back to college to receive enhanced education (Bachelor's in Nursing), or if I should continue earning money. During this era of contemplation, with much prayer and thought, I decided to receive more education.

While pondering upon my decision, I came across this passage of scripture: "Seek not for riches but for wisdom."[68]

When I read that passage, the Spirit touched my heart. I felt the confirmation that the decision to go back to school to receive more "wisdom" was the correct choice. I literally cannot imagine my life without the experiences, opportunities, and lifelong friendships I gained through the choice to go back to college.

The prophet, Spencer W. Kimball, taught that as we study the scriptures and apply them to our lives, "We shall find answers to our problems and peace in our hearts."[69] *Steadfastly hold to the word of God!*

<u>Example 3</u>

My sister-in-law, Darci, was having a tough time deciding if she, and her husband (my brother, Jason), should have more children. Much prayer was lifted up to the Lord for help to do what was right.

With her specific question in mind, she continued to read the scriptures daily. She also delved into articles in the *Ensign* magazine (this magazine contains the monthly teachings of the modern-day prophets), and other spiritual resources. As she read, she felt peace, but uncertainty. At times, she felt like there was no direct answer. It was frustrating. She was willing to do whatever the Lord asked, so why wouldn't He just tell her what to do?! Have you ever felt that way? It can be tough.

---

[68] *Doctrine and Covenants* 11:7; *Doctrine and Covenants* 9:8-9.
[69] Spencer W. Kimball, *The Teachings of Spencer W. Kimball*, ed. Edward L. Kimball [1982], 129, 135.

Finally, with consistent effort on her part, she came across an article that reiterated this teaching:

> Our Heavenly Father may answer prayers in a wide variety of ways other than a simple "yes" or "no." For example, when we have properly prepared ourselves to receive and accept his counsel, he might lead us to a scripture offering the very answer we need. When there seems to be no clear-cut "yes" or "no" answer to a question asked in prayer, it may be that either choice is acceptable.[70]

Elder Robert D. Hales powerfully taught:

> When we want to speak to God, we pray. And when we want Him to speak to us, we search the scriptures; for His words are spoken through His prophets. He will then teach us as we listen to the promptings of the Holy Spirit.[71]

Through the Lord's teachings and the scriptures, she was able to find the peace and understanding that either choice was a righteous decision. *Steadfastly hold to the word of God!*

Example 4

I imagine that we all go through stages in which we question our self-worth. I was going through a hard time wondering if the Lord was aware of me. During that period in my life, President Dieter F. Uchtdorf delivered a talk called: "Forget Me Not." *Steadfastly hold to the word of God!*

This talk poured sweet consolation into my soul. It was like a telegram to Kayla, from Heavenly Father, telling me that I was not forgotten. God answered my prayers through one of His modern-day apostles. One of the divine truths taught in this talk included:

---

[70] Grant E. Barton, "Discerning Answers to Our Prayers," *Ensign*, Feb. 1996, The Church of Jesus Christ of Latter-day Saints, Feb. 1996 (accessed Aug. 2, 2016).
[71] Robert D. Hales, "Holy Scriptures: The Power of God unto Our Salvation," *Ensign*, Nov. 2006, 24-27.

Whatever your circumstances may be, you are not forgotten. No matter how dark your days may seem, no matter how insignificant you may feel, no matter how overshadowed you think you may be, your Heavenly Father has not forgotten you. In fact, He loves you with an infinite love.

Just think of it: You are known and remembered by the most majestic, powerful, and glorious Being in the universe! You are loved by the King of infinite space and everlasting time! He who created and knows the stars knows you and your name—you are [a child] of His kingdom.[72]

The Lord speaks to us through His apostles and prophets today just as in days of old. *Steadfastly hold to the word of God!*

A modern-day apostle, President Marion G. Romney declared:

I feel certain that if, in our homes, parents will read from the Book of Mormon prayerfully and regularly, both by themselves and with their children, the spirit of that great book will come to permeate our homes and all who dwell therein…The spirit of contention will depart. Parents will counsel their children in greater love and wisdom. Children will be more responsive and submissive to the counsel of their parents. Righteousness will increase. Faith, hope, and charity—the pure love of Christ—will abound in our homes and lives, bringing in their wake peace, joy, and happiness.[73]

The prophet, Ezra T. Benson, reminded us:

One of the most important things you can do…is to immerse yourselves in the scriptures. Search them

[72] Dieter F. Uchtdorf, "Forget Me Not," *Ensign*, Nov. 2011, 120-123.
[73] Marion G. Romney, "The Book of Mormon," *Ensign*, May 1980, *lds.org*, The Church of Jesus Christ of Latter-day Saints, Nov. 1980 (accessed Jan. 8, 2017).

diligently. Feast upon the words of Christ. Learn the doctrine. Master the principles that are found therein. Few other efforts will bring greater dividends…Few other ways [will result in] greater inspiration.

You must…see that studying and searching the scriptures is not a burden laid upon [us] by the Lord, but a marvelous blessing and opportunity.[74]

President Benson also gave this heart-piercing promise:

There is a power in the [Book of Mormon] which will begin to flow into your lives the minute you begin a serious study of the book. You will find greater power to resist temptation. You will find the power to avoid deception. You will find the power to stay on the strait and narrow path. When you begin to hunger and thirst after those words, you will find life in greater and greater abundance.[75]

When we feel lost in life's journey, or when we want to become a better person, or when we want to feel peace, we must remember that we have something tangible, sturdy, and reliable that we can hold on to that will give us clarity, divine help, and peace. This firm resource is the iron rod. The mists of darkness, worldly voices, and threatening rivers are real and menacing. As we hold steadfastly to the iron rod, we will overcome the obstacles we will face in life and we will not be deceived.[76] Let us use the scriptures, apply them, love them, and thank our loving God for them. Start somewhere; start today! *Steadfastly hold to the word of God!*

Perhaps you noticed how strongly intertwined scripture study and prayer are with each other. That leads us directly to our next Star!

---

[74] Ezra T. Benson, "The Power of the Word," *Ensign*, May 1986, 81.
[75] "President Ezra Taft Benson: A Sure Voice of Faith," *Ensign*, July 1994, p. 11.
[76] *Joseph Smith-Matthew* 1:37; 1 Nephi 15:24; Thomas S. Monson, "The Power of the Book of Mormon," *Ensign*, May 2017, *lds.org*, The Church of Jesus Christ of Latter-day Saints, May 2017 (accessed May 4, 2017).

Chapter 5

5 Star Day:

Sincere Prayer

WHEN I WAS a young child, I was taught by my parents how to pray. We prayed as a family in the morning, at night, and during meals—so I had plenty of opportunities to practice. I was taught that Heavenly Father heard my prayers and that He would answer them.

As a little girl, I recall kneeling at my bedside one night, giving a simple child's prayer. As I closed this particular prayer, I stopped, squinted one eye toward heaven, and concluded, "And please bless that I can get one million dollars." Upon finishing my prayer, my childlike innocence was firm, but I felt kind of silly. So I added, "And I'll use it to help other people." I am sure Heavenly Father got a good chuckle that night. I did not get one million dollars, but I could feel that Heavenly Father was listening.

God does hear and answer our prayers, and He longs for us to communicate with Him. It is important to ask the right questions when we pray. It is equally important to remember that our timing is not always the same as the Lord's timing when it comes to receiving answers to our supplications. Sometimes this fact can be trying, but we can remember that the Lord has our best interest in mind.

One of the earliest experiences I can recall with Sincere Prayer was when I was about eight years of age. I opened the garage door and I saw that my dad, Kimball, was working hard to fix our big family Suburban on our driveway. The car would not start, and his face reflected frustration. I knew if the car did not work our family's schedule would be greatly interrupted.

I closed the garage door and snuck around the corner into our little laundry room. I knelt down and offered a sincere prayer to our Father in Heaven—thanking Him for my family and for our car. I then pleaded for His help to fix it. Shortly following, I heard a noise. I opened the garage door once again. I can still see in my mind's eye our big Suburban driving around the block.

Perhaps you can relate to similar experiences with sincere prayer. Examples may include: finding lost keys, coming upon missing toys or little shoes, or arriving at a destination after being lost. The Lord is aware of even the simplest things. Sincerity in our prayers includes not only praying in time of need, but praying fervently daily—in the rainy seasons of life as well as the sunny ones.

Why is Sincere Prayer so vital in our lives that it merits a Star in the 5 Star Day? Prayer is the most basic form of personal worship. We do not need to go to the temple or the church to do it. No matter what our spiritual state be, prayer is available to us at any time. It is our choice to access this amazing power.

It has been noted by leaders of the church and many religious scholars that the divine invitation to pray unto the Father in the name of Jesus Christ is the single most mentioned commandment in all recorded scripture. The most! Elder Kevin W. Pearson gives us perspective as to why:

> Prayer is an essential and enabling spiritual link between God and man. Without prayer, there is no possible return

to the Father. Without prayer, sufficient faith to understand and keep the commandments is impossible. Without prayer, the necessary spiritual power to avoid temptation and overcome trials and adversity would be unavailable. Without prayer, repentance, forgiveness and the cleansing power of [His] Atonement are unattainable. With the power of personal prayer, all things are possible.[1]

What about when we feel far from God, or when we feel we are not ready to pray? First of all, remember that "if ye would hearken unto the Spirit which teacheth a man to pray, ye would know that ye must pray; for the evil spirit teacheth not a man to pray."[2] We can take baby steps in this process. Elder Richard G. Scott taught:

Your access to the Savior's help comes in different ways. The most direct and often the most powerful way is through humble, trusting prayers to your Father in Heaven, which are answered through the Holy Ghost to your spirit. Yet this help is sometimes difficult to initiate and hard to recognize when you are learning how to pray with faith. If so, begin elsewhere. Trust someone near to you; then as you learn, that trust will extend to God and His healing. Begin with a friend or bishop who understands the teachings of the Savior. Often they have personally obtained healing through application of truth with faith in the Redeemer. They can show you how. Or start by reading, pondering, and applying the teachings of the scriptures. They are a very powerful source of assistance.[3]

Also take into account these insightful teachings by the prophet Thomas S. Monson:

---

[1] Kevin W. Pearson, "Improving Your Personal Prayers," *Ensign*, June 2013, 36-39.
[2] 2 Nephi 32:8-9.
[3] Richard G. Scott, "To Be Healed," *Ensign*, May 1994, *lds.org*, The Church of Jesus Christ of Latter-day Saints, May 1994 (accessed July 10, 2016).

As we offer unto the Lord our family prayers and our personal prayers, let us do so with faith and trust in Him. If any of us has been slow to hearken to the counsel to pray always, there is no finer hour to begin than now. Those who feel that prayer might denote a physical or intellectual weakness should remember that a man never stands taller than when he is upon his knees.[4]

Many artists have created depictions of the Lord knocking outside a door that contains no external handle. This artwork is portraying the subtle yet powerful symbolism that we need to let Him in. "Behold, I stand at the door, and knock: if any man hear my voice, and open the door, I will come in to him, and will sup with him, and he with me."[5] President Boyd K. Packer relates, "Prayer is your personal key to heaven. The lock is on your side of the veil."[6]

How Can We Enhance the Sincerity in Our Prayers?

Prayer has three parts much like a sandwich—yummy yummy. We begin by (1) addressing Heavenly Father (first slice of bread). Then we (2) express gratitude, ask for guidance, pray for others, and talk to Him openly (various ingredients we put on the sandwich). We then (3) finish our prayer "in the name of Jesus Christ, amen" (finishing slice of bread).

The word "Sincere" is the most important part of the Sincere Prayer Star. A routine prayer with superficial phases may technically be defined as "saying a prayer," but is that what the Lord is asking when He commands us to "counsel with the Lord in all thy doings," and to "pray unto the Father with all the energy of heart"?[7]

---

[4] Thomas S. Monson, "Come unto Him in Prayer and Faith," *Ensign*, March 2009, 5-9.
[5] Revelation 3:20.
[6] Boyd K. Packer, "Personal Revelation: The Gift, the Test, and the Promise," *Ensign*, Nov. 1994, 59.
[7] Alma 37:37; Moroni 7:48.

Sincere prayer is a two-way communication. It is like a telephone call with Heavenly Father. Our wonderful "prayer phone" comes with unlimited minutes and it is free. No catch. When we remember that it is our loving Heavenly Dad on the other end of the line, and that we are one of His precious children, "then at once prayer becomes natural and instinctive on our part."[8] The Bible Dictionary teaches that "many of the so-called difficulties about prayer arise from forgetting this relationship."[9]

However, the prayer phone analogy must be used carefully. We ought to be having quality exchanges with our Father, and sincerity is definitely the key. President Gordon B. Hinckley observed:

> The trouble with most of our prayers is that we give them as if we were picking up the telephone and ordering groceries—we place our order and hang up. We need to meditate, contemplate, think of what we are praying about and for and then speak to the Lord as one man speaketh to another.[10]

We are typically not going to hear the Lord's literal voice like we would on the phone; He speaks in a different way. Prayer involves all three members of the Godhead. We pray to Heavenly Father in the name of Jesus Christ by the power of the Holy Ghost.[11] God answers our prayers through the Holy Ghost. President Boyd K. Packer taught that the Holy Ghost is "felt rather than heard."[12] The recognition of these feelings requires moments of being still and listening with our hearts and minds during and after our prayers.

Another important key to this communication is choosing to let our will align with the Lord's will.[13] When we have that perspective in mind, a tangible power is felt in our prayers and in our lives.

---

[8] *Bible Dictionary*: Prayer.
[9] *Bible Dictionary*: Prayer.
[10] Gordon B. Hinckley, *Stand Ye in Holy Places*, 1974, 244.
[11] 3 Nephi 19:6; Moroni 8:8; 3 Nephi 18:21; John 14:13; John 16:23; Romans 8:26; Psalm 46:1.
[12] Boyd K. Packer, "Counsel to the Youth," *Ensign*, Nov. 2011, 17.
[13] *Bible Dictionary*: Prayer; Luke 22:42; John 15:7; *Doctrine and Covenants* 109:44.

Mary Jane Woodger, a religion teacher, once suggested that we express a "reality statement" to Heavenly Father, such as: "I'm lonely," "I'm depleted of energy," "My friend, John, is losing hope." She has experienced that her prayers are intensified when she does this. She noted that the Savior Himself used a reality statement in Gethsemane as He pled, "Let this cup pass."[14] Then Christ chose to obey God's will on our behalf.

Sister Woodger taught, "For me, habitual phrases such as 'bless my family' or 'help me' do not usually constitute mighty prayer. My prayers are more effective when they include names and circumstances."[15]

With these strategies in mind, it is important that we talk about two essential actions that help us more fully feel the Lord's touch through prayer: being prepared and staying focused.

Being Prepared and Staying Focused

What would listening to your personal prayers reveal about you and your relationship with Heavenly Father? I admit that I have had many, many, yep, many prayers that have gone something like this:

The alarm clock beeps, and the beast awakens. A sound, much like a dinosaur's roar, echoes across the valley as the beast pulls off her bedsheets and sits on the side of her bed. She knows how important it is to pray in the morning, so she slumps over like a plop of mashed potatoes onto the floor. She begins to mutter rehearsed prayer phrases—while slowly fading back into a deep abyss of unconsciousness. Once the beast reopens her eyes (after who knows how long), she looks around the room, in a disoriented gaze, only to end her prayer with an "Amen?"

Okay, that was pretty dramatic, but I am just being honest that sometimes it is hard to stay focused while we pray. Preparation is a

---

14 Matthew 26:39.
15 Mary Jane Woodger, "What I have Learned About Mighty Prayer," *Ensign*, Dec. 2006, *lds.org*, The Church of Jesus Christ of Latter-day Saints, Dec. 2006 (accessed August 3, 2016).

divine help for that common problem. For example, the recent story about the grumpy tired Kayla was a pretty typical morning for me growing up. As an adolescent, I knew I needed to make a switch. After pondering on and studying the subject, I learned that I needed to prepare myself before making a supplication to the Lord. So I began experimenting different things.

With time, I found it was helpful for me to go the bathroom and wash my face first thing after waking up. A sticky note was placed on my bathroom mirror with the reminder to pray. With my brain more alert, I returned to my bedside with my lights on much more ready to make a sincere prayer. I invite you to experiment different techniques that help you stay more alert during your prayers.

During a religion class, a female peer once shared the meaningful way she chose to prepare herself for her personal prayers. She would close her eyes and quietly imagining this scenario:

In her mind's eye, she imagines walking up to a desk. The secretary asks sweetly, "Can I help you?" My friend then responds, "Yes, I've come to meet with my Dad." The secretary then looks at some papers, and says, "Father is ready to see you now." They enter into an exquisitely white room that could be compared to the Celestial Room in holy temples. Seated on His throne in the middle of this familiar room sits Heavenly Father. The secretary then smiles and leaves the room.

After visualizing this scenario, she mentally approaches God's throne and humbly begins her prayer. My sister, Janessa, is another person who has spoken of this method.

Since hearing of this scenario, I have experimented with this method as a means for preparing for personal prayer, and it is has completely changed my prayers. My prayer is always directed toward Heavenly Father, but I like to imagine Heavenly Mother seated next to Him intently listening during my prayer. I also picture the Savior there; sometimes He sits by me, and other times He sits next to

Heavenly Father.[16] This image makes the sacred communication of prayer feel even more real to me.

Pondering and preparing beforehand the things we need to talk to Heavenly Father about helps us stay focused during communion with our Creator.[17]

The scriptures mention that "we know not what we should pray for as we ought."[18] In my early college years, I was taught by my sister, Ashton, the power of asking for help in our prayers to know what to pray for. I recall the first night I experimented with this counsel. I had a pretty routine prayer and was about to finish, but then I stopped myself and asked, "Dear Father in Heaven, will you please help me know what else I ought to pray for tonight?" The Holy Ghost began to place subtle thoughts into my mind, turning my prayer into supplications for individuals and situations that I would not have prayed for on my own. When my prayer was closed, I remember kneeling for a while in awe of how aware the Lord was of me and others. I learned that we never know who is praying for us by name. This method also keeps us focused.

Another useful method of preparation is one learned from my dad, Kimball, in using technology as a resource to remind us to pray. He sets a reminder prompt that displays on his computer screen. This simple computer reminder helps ensure that he says a prayer each day personally and with his spouse. Sometimes we forget to start the day out right. Cell phones or handheld devices can also easily be used for sending important reminders.

Preparation and focus gain greater power as we fast. Fasting (to go without food/drink for two consecutive meals) is a divine gift and commandment from God.[19] This spiritual practice is physically

[16] "The Family: A Proclamation to the World," *lds.org*; "Mother in Heaven," *lds.org/topics*; (both accessed Feb. 7, 2016); "O My Father," *Hymns*, no. 292.
[17] 3 Nephi 13:5-8; Matthew 7:7-11; Ephesians 6:18.
[18] Romans 8:26.
[19] Alma 5:45-46; Isaiah 58; Matthew 6:16-18; *Doctrine and Covenants* 88:76; Mosiah 27:22-23.

based, but it gives us huge spiritual benefit. We can overcome weaknesses and confirm truth through fasting and prayer. Similarly, we may fast and pray for help and guidance on behalf of others who may be ill or struggling.[20]

It is much easier to receive personal revelation for the questions that we have in the gospel, and in life in general, when we have prepared ourselves and stayed focus.

Personal Revelation

Personal revelation is one of the greatest gifts that we can receive. It includes individual guidance, counsel, and direction from the Lord. Elder Kevin W. Pearson taught:

> Inspired questions bring greater focus, purpose, and meaning to our prayers. If you want to receive more personal revelation through your prayers, you may want to think about what questions you are asking. Revelation generally comes in response to a question. The process of revelation requires us to search the scriptures, ponder them, and apply them to our lives. As we do so, the Holy Ghost helps us form inspired questions.[21]

Typically we want an answer to come right now! That cannot be our usual experience, however. The Lord knows that we grow as we work to receive answers to our questions. President Boyd. K. Packer said:

> The answer may not come as a lightning bolt. It may come as a little inspiration here and a little there, "line upon line, precept upon precept" (D&C 98:12). Some answers will come from reading the scriptures, some from hearing

[20] *Gospel Principles*, The Church of Jesus Christ of Latter-day Saints (2011), 144-48; Carl B. Pratt, "Blessings of a Proper Fast," *Ensign*, Oct. 2004, *lds.org*, The Church of Jesus Christ of Latter-day Saints, Oct. 2004 (accessed March 27, 2017).
[21] Kevin W. Pearson, "Improving Your Personal Prayers," *Ensign*, June 2013, 36-39.

speakers. And, occasionally, when it is important, some will come by very direct and powerful inspiration.[22]

Elder David A. Bednar taught that the "light" of revelation is most typically received like "the rising sun" (gradually) or like the light during a "foggy day" (you can see just enough ahead of you to take a few steps of faith).[23] If you have a personal question, you have all the tools necessary to get a personal answer. Personal revelation includes obtaining direction to know what the Lord would have you do today to serve those around you (see Chapter 6).

As we take moments to *listen* and to *feel His love* during prayer, we can come to experience His guidance in our lives. We can also take inventory of what we have done throughout the day. During my evening prayer, I like to ask myself, "Did I truly strive to have a 5 Star Day today?" Then I go over each Star, and think about my efforts made, God's help, things I learned, and how I can be an instrument in His hands the next day. Personal revelation is a gift.

Getting to the Point of Praying Always

The habit of praying on our knees—morning and night—is important. We ought to kneel in prayer daily as individuals, as couples, and as families.[24] In addition to that, we are commanded that we should "pray always to the Father in the name of the Son."[25]

We clearly cannot kneel at our bedside and pray all day long, nor should we walk around the streets praying vocally every minute. Clearly fasting is an extremely important friend of the Sincere Prayer Star, but we cannot fast and pray 24/7 or else we will die. So how can we develop the Sincere Prayer Star in our lives to the point of fulfilling the mandate to pray always?

---

[22] Boyd K. Packer, "Prayers and Answers," *Ensign*, Oct. 1979, *lds.org* (accessed July 17, 2016).
[23] David A. Bednar, "The Spirit of Revelation," *Ensign*, May 2011, 87-89.
[24] 3 Nephi 19:8; 3 Nephi 1:11; Acts 7:60; Alma 34:27; Acts 9:40; Acts 21:5; Alma 46:13.
[25] 3 Nephi 18:19-20; Ephesians 6:18; Luke 21:36; Alma 34:27.

We can communicate with Heavenly Father vocally or silently. Silent prayers can take place when we are in the midst of our daily tasks. We do this by quietly directing expressions and thoughts in our minds and hearts toward God.[26]

In the Book of Mormon, the people of Alma engaged in silent prayer when they were prohibited from praying vocally by King Amulon: "Alma and his people did not raise their voices to the Lord their God, but did pour out their hearts to him; and he did know the thoughts of their hearts."[27]

A talk given by Elder David A. Bednar on the matter of "praying always" had a positive impact on my life. He spoke of how the Lord showed us an important pattern during the creation of the world. In the scriptures we read: "For I, the Lord God, created all things, of which I have spoken, spiritually, before they were naturally upon the face of the earth."[28] Practically every scriptural miracle was wrought after a prayer was said.[29] Elder Bednar gave us further insight:

> Meaningful morning prayer is an important element in the spiritual creation of each day—and precedes the temporal creation or the actual execution of the day…Morning and evening prayers—and all of the prayers in between—are not unrelated, discrete events; rather, they are linked together each day and across days, weeks, months, and even years. This is in part how we fulfill the scriptural admonition to pray always.[30]

What great perspective! We ought to begin our mornings with a more purposeful prayer relating to that specific day. With the directive to first "spiritually create our day," we can then see the

---

[26] Alma 37:36; Mosiah 26:39.
[27] Mosiah 24:12.
[28] Moses 3:4-5.
[29] Number 21:6-9; 2 Kings 20:1-6; Jeremiah 29:13; Daniel 6:10-23; Jonah 2:7-10; Matthew 17:14-21; Matthew 21:20-21; Matthew 26:39; Luke 9:28-36; Enos 1; Mosiah 24:12-14; Mark 6:47-43; 1 Nephi 16:23-32; *Joseph Smith-History* 1:13-20; *Doctrine and Covenants* 35; *Doctrine and Covenants* 91; etc.
[30] David A. Bednar, "Pray Always," *Ensign*, Nov. 2008, 41-43.

"physical creation" that follows. Wherever we abide, we will be able to see the world in a holier sphere. We can be walking in the crisp morning air, and choose to see the beautiful sunshine as it seeps through the leaves of the trees.

Similarly, the choice to "create" a smile on someone's face as we pass them becomes a physical creation that we produced. We can "create" a new friendship while we are standing in the grocery line, or sit by someone at school who looks like they need a lift. Prayer in our hearts for the people we brush shoulders with can be a day-to-day occurrence as we go about our tasks. As we finish the routines of our day and retire to our designated spot to say our evening prayer, hopefully we will be able to feel that we have been in communion with God throughout the entire day. As that cycle continues, we will have continual correspondence.

The times in my life when my communion with God is like the examples I just shared, I feel a dominant peacefulness that enhances all aspects of my existence.

I am sorry to say that there have been many phases in my life when I have—little-by-little—gone back to making less sincere prayers, and my life is not nearly as fulfilling or joyful. When I get back into the habit of consistent communion with God, that sweet power returns. *Sincerity is the key!*

Sincere Prayer in Action

Example 1

One of the most unexpected experiences I have had with the Sincere Prayer Star took place while I was working in a hospital as a nurse. I was taking care of an elderly lady who had broken her hip and was in a lot of pain. Throughout my shift she would express her beliefs in God, and we had several spiritual chats.

77

During one of our interactions, she confided in me that she had been praying on behalf of some of her family members who were in tough situations. I felt comfortable—within the lines of professional boundaries—relating to her a hard situation that was currently going on in my life.

One of my loved ones was struggling with severe emotional and mental challenges. As I expressed this concern to her, she said to me, "Well, by golly, let's pray!" Initially, I just sat and stared at her, thinking she was potentially joking. She was not.

What seemed like a "movie moment" angelic gesture, she slowly held out her feeble hands to take mine. In a whisper, she quoted a scripture to me, "Kayla, where two or three are gathered together in His name, His power may be manifested."[31] Even as I write about this experience right now, my insides churn with emotion. I cannot express the grace this precious woman showed as she took my hands in hers, and lifted up one of the deepest and sincerest prayers on behalf of my loved one—someone whom she had never met.

By the end of her supplication, we were both crying. I gave her a hug, and I thanked her for the sincere prayer. She replied, "Kayla, I'm a Prayer Warrior! The sweet Lord has given us the opportunity to communicate with Him at any time. My heart is filled with the desire to pray for others." *Sincerity is the key!*

Example 2

I need to explain a few things before I relate this wonderful story about sincere prayer. So far in this book, I have mentioned the word *missionaries* a few times. The glorious news of the restoration of the Lord's gospel is to be shared with the entire world—even until it has reached every nation, kindred, tongue, and people.[32]

---

[31] Matthew 18:20.
[32] Revelations 14:6-7; 2 Nephi 26:13; Mosiah 3:13&20; Alma 37:4; Isaiah 61:1; Mark 16:15.

In The Church of Jesus Christ of Latter-day Saints, young men and women (typically in their early twenties) can choose to set aside eighteen months (for women or "Sisters") to two years (for men or "Elders") of their lives to do nothing else but invite others to come unto Christ by helping them to take the necessary steps to return home (Chapter 2).[33] Serving a mission requires hard work 24/7! It is not a study abroad or a vacation; it is a divine calling. Missionaries are "set apart," or granted the Lord's authority, to preach Christ's gospel.[34] Through revelation received by God's apostles, these young men and women are assigned where to labor.[35] They teach the gospel in rotating pairs, referred to as "companionships."[36]

There is no calling or ministry in the church that receives wages in exchange for their service, and missionaries are no exception. Missionaries pay to serve, and it is so worth it. I chose to serve a mission, and the Lord called me to labor in Neuquén, Argentina, for eighteen months.

While serving in Argentina, my companion and I learned of the profound effect the members of the church have in inviting others to come unto Christ. In fact, as everyday members, our ability to aid in the Lord's work of spreading His gospel is just as great—and in some ways greater—than that of the missionaries.

My companion and I worked with all our might to help the members feel this divine calling to invite the people around them to learn about the gospel. We visited home after home of church members with families of all types. Some had parents with young kids and others had parents with grown kids. Several homes were single parents raising their children, while a few others were single adults that lived alone. No matter the family circumstances, they all

---

[33] Matthew 3:2; Mosiah 23:17; 3 Nephi 20:30-31; *Doctrine and Covenants* 18:41-42; *Doctrine and Covenants* 123:12.
[34] *Doctrine and Covenants* 1:23; *Articles of Faith* 1:5; Isaiah 61:1; *Doctrine and Covenants* 42:11; Ezekiel 34:11; *Doctrine and Covenants* 29:7.
[35] Ronald A. Rasband, "The Divine Call of a Missionary," *Ensign*, May 2010, 51-53.
[36] Isaiah 52:7; *Doctrine and Covenants* 18:13-17; Matthew 24:14; *Doctrine and Covenants* 42:6.

had the same mandate and ability to share the gospel with those around them.

We arrived, one late afternoon, to the home of an elderly sister. As we entered her humble house, there was nothing elegant or extravagant about her living situation. However, as we crammed around her tiny table, we felt at home. We could feel the Holy Ghost. The Spirit is what made her small, damp house a home.

As we shared the words of the Savior and the examples of great missionaries of old, we all began to be edified. She shared with us the turning point of her own conversion, bore testimony of what God had done for her, and acknowledged that the Lord is aware of all His children. By the end of her conversion story, our cheeks were wet with tears.

My companion and I then delivered the challenge the Lord wanted us to give: "Dear sister, we know there are people around you today who are ready to receive the gospel. The Lord will bless and guide you to know who they are. Will you help someone in your life to the waters of baptism within six weeks?" With tears in her eyes, this dear sister did not hesitate. She replied, "Yes, sisters…I will. I owe it to my great Lord and Savior. He has done so much for me."

We were humbled by her faith and asked her if we could kneel in prayer. We inquired if she would be willing to offer the prayer, and she gladly accepted. As we knelt, huddled together on her cold, wet floor, we encouraged her to ask specifically to be guided to that individual who was ready to receive the gospel.

We closed our eyes and bowed our heads as this sweet sister lifted up a prayer that was so humble, powerful, and sincere that the very frame of my body did quake. With tears in her eyes, she begged to be guided and able to share Christ's divine gospel with someone. She spoke to Heavenly Father as her Almighty God, Creator, and

Father. I knew that very day that the Lord would answer her prayer and that she would be guided to someone ready to be baptized.

Through her diligence, and by the hand of God, she was. She began to have recurring thoughts about a family friend. Through her friendship and invitation, this family friend did indeed receive the gospel and was baptized within six weeks. Over time, an amazing chain-reaction has taken place. Many loved ones of that baptized individual have also made covenants with the Lord. *Sincerity is the key!*

<u>Example 3</u>

We see many examples of Sincere Prayer in the holy scriptures. Christ was the perfect example, lifting up prayers of pure gratitude often and typically a miracle followed afterward.[37] He also gave the example of proper prayer form: kneeling, and addressing Heavenly Father. Then praying for things such as: the will of God to be done, forgiveness, help with our daily needs, divine protection from the devil, and acknowledging the glory of God.[38]

Christ exhorted that we not use "vain repetitions" (insincerely saying the same things over and over) in prayer, and that we ought to "pray in secret."[39] Now, that does not mean that we should not pray in our congregations or out loud. Rather, we should be sincere and personal in our communication with the Father. We should not pray to "be seen of men."[40] *Sincerity is the key!*

Can you feel the difference between Prayer versus Sincere Prayer and see why the "S" part of the 5 Star Day is the word "Sincere"?

---

[37] Matthew 15:32-38; Matthew 11:25; 3 Nephi 19:20-28.
[38] 3 Nephi 13:9-13; Matthew 6:9-13.
[39] Matthew 6:5-8.
[40] Matthew 6:5.

Many parts of the scriptures teach helpful tools that enhance our prayers.[41] The incredible missionaries, Alma and Amulek, taught:

> Yea, and when you do not cry unto the Lord [vocally], let your hearts be full, drawn out in prayer unto him continually for your welfare, and also for the welfare of those who are around you.[42]

Directly following these insights, the next verse teaches us the crucial correlation between prayer and action:

> I say unto you, do not suppose that this is all; for after ye have done all these things, if ye turn away the needy, and the naked, and visit not the sick and afflicted, and impart of your substance, if ye have, to those who stand in need—I say unto you, *if ye do not any of these things, behold, your prayer is vain, and availeth you nothing,* and ye are as hypocrites who do deny the faith.[43]

Turns out, after we hone in on the power of prayer, we must go from our knees to our feet. Without action following prayer, we will not obtain the growing and wonderful experiences the Lord intends for us to have. My sister-in-law, Darci, shared with me a poem that enhanced my views on this subject. The divine parallel between prayer and action is taught powerfully with these words:

I knelt to pray when day was done
And prayed, "O Lord, bless everyone,
Lift from each saddened heart the pain
And let the sick be well again."
And then I woke another day
And carelessly went on my way,
The whole day long I did not try
To wipe a tear from any eye.
I did not try to share the load

---

[41] Alma 37:36-37; *Doctrine and Covenants* 10:5; Matthew 7:7-8; 1 Nephi 17:7; Mosiah 24:12; Enos 1.
[42] Alma 34:18-27; comment added.
[43] Alma 34:28; emphasis added.

Of any brother on the road.
I did not even go to see
The sick man just next door to me.
Yet once again when day was done
I prayed, "O Lord, bless everyone."
But as I prayed, into my ear
there came a voice that whispered clear,
"Pause now, my son, before you pray.
Whom have you tried to bless today?
Gods sweetest blessing always go
by hands that serve him here below."
And then I hid my face and cried,
"Forgive me, God, I have not tried,
But let me live another day
and I will live the way I pray."[44]

As a review, we apply the Sincere Prayer Star at a deeper level through preparing, staying focused, and striving to receive personal revelation. Praying always is a divine commandment and our goal. The Lord would not give any commandment that is not for our joy and divine help. God wants us to communicate with Him because we are important to Him. Let's show Him that He is important to us. Prayer gives us enhanced help and direction from above; this changes everything. Just like this poem and last scripture testified, the Sincere Prayer Star is directly linked to action.

This leads us straight to our next Star (woot woot!).

---

[44] Unknown Author, "The Way I Pray," *insighttools.net/faith* (accessed July 30, 2016).

Chapter 6

5 Star Day:

Service

I WILL ADMIT THAT working as a nurse has been one of the hardest, greatest, and most humbling experiences of my life. I am amazed by people. While there is much pain and suffering in this life, there is also so much good. The positive is worth fighting for.

For my first job as a nurse, I worked at a nursing home. Though this opportunity was emotionally and physically demanding, I would never trade the things I learned while working there. And more than anything, I cherish the angelic moments I witnessed among these precious patients who were in such a lonely phase of their lives.

One of my patients was very hard of hearing and was losing her memory at a rapid rate. Due to her memory loss, she had a difficult time expressing words. Despite her challenges, she would always say "thank you" after any act of kindness or care given to her.

Another patient experienced chronic pain and had to spend a lot of time resting in her bed. However, at least once a week she would ask me to push her in her wheelchair from room to room so that she could check up on the other residents, offering them comfort.

It can be so easy to forget the impact that simple, genuine acts of kindness can have on the lives of those around us. Small gestures of compassion can cause a positive ripple effect in the world.

I believe that this experience shared in the inspirational book, *Rediscover Jesus*, gives us perspective on how God feels about daily sincere service:

> It was the biggest meeting of Paul's life, and it had gone well. He couldn't wait to tell his wife and his boss. As he rushed out of the Brooklyn office building with the rest of the team, they noticed a vacant cab—a rare sight during rush hour.
>
> Eager to get to the airport to catch their flight home, they bolted toward the cab, yelling to get the driver's attention. But as they made their way across the sidewalk, they inadvertently knocked over a small produce stand. The rest of the team seemed oblivious until Paul stopped and turned around to go back.
>
> From beside the taxi the others called out to Paul. "Come on, you'll miss your flight."
>
> "Go ahead without me," Paul replied as he made his way back across the street toward the sidewalk covered in produce. At that moment, he realized that the woman who had been behind the produce stand was blind. She was just standing there crying softly with tears running down her face.
>
> "It's OK. It's OK," Paul said to her as he got down on his hands and knees and began picking up the fruit and vegetables. There were a hundred people passing in each direction, but nobody else stopped to help. They just scurried off to wherever they were going.
>
> When the fruit was all back up on the stand, Paul began neatly organizing it, setting aside anything that was spoiled. Now he turned to the woman and asked, "Are you OK?" She nodded through her tears. Then, reaching for his wallet,

he took out some bills and passed them to the woman, saying, "This money should cover the damages."

With that, Paul turned and began to walk away.

"Mister," the woman called after him. Paul paused and turned around. "Are you Jesus?"

"Oh no," he replied.

The woman nodded and continued, "I only ask because I prayed for Jesus to help me as I heard my fruit falling all over the sidewalk."

Paul turned to leave again, only now his eyes began to fill with tears.

For a long time he wandered around looking for a taxi. After finally finding one, he sat in bumper-to-bumper traffic all the way to the airport. He had missed his flight, and because it was Friday night, all other flights were full.

Paul spent the night in a hotel by the airport. This gave him time to think. He couldn't get one question out of his head: *When was the last time someone confused you for Jesus?*[1]

Tears often swell up in my eyes when I read this story. That question truly pierces the heart. When was the last time someone confused you for Jesus? I would like to add, when was the last time you asked yourself, "What would Jesus do if He were here?"

Genuine kindness truly makes a difference. I will be bold enough to say it makes *all* the difference in our homes, careers, relationships, and lives in general. The prophet, Alma, taught (Book of Mormon):

> Therefore, my son, see that you are merciful unto your brethren; deal justly, judge righteously, and do good continually; and if ye do all these things then shall ye receive your reward; yea, ye shall have mercy restored unto you again; ye shall have justice restored unto you again; ye shall have a righteous judgment restored unto you again; and ye shall have good rewarded unto you again.

[1] Matthew Kelly, *Rediscover Jesus*, Prologue, 2015; emphasis added.

For that which ye do send out shall return unto you again, and be restored.[2]

In our day-to-day interactions with others, what are we "sending out" into the world? Are we sending out anger, rudeness, negativity, unrighteous judgement, and hate? Or are we sending out patience, kindness, righteous judgement, and love? I have seen the pattern that this scripture reveals in my own life and in the lives of others. As we genuinely choose to be kind and to love, that kindness and love generally returns unto our own lives often.

In this process of sending out genuine kindness, love, and hope in Christ into the world, there is a connection between discipleship, charity, and service. The relationship between these three principles is the foundation of the Service Star.

Discipleship, Charity, and Service

To be considered a disciple of Jesus Christ—a true and honest follower of Him—is one of the greatest compliments that can be given in this life. In relation to discipleship, a modern-day apostle, Elder M. Russell Ballard, gave a parable about a wealthy prospector.

The career of the prospector was to dig for gold, which had the potential to make him rich. This prospector was well-off because he was wise and diligent. He patiently gathered *daily golden flecks* instead of waiting for large gold nuggets. This persevering accumulation of flecks resulted in great riches for the intelligent prospector. The individuals who focused only on large gold nuggets came up empty most of the time, and this result led to frustration and giving up.[3]

As we genuinely serve others, these actions are molding us in our journey of life to become golden and refined ourselves, even true

---

[2] Alma 41:14-15.
[3] M. Russell Ballard, "Finding Joy Through Loving Service," *Ensign*, May 2011, 46-49; see Matthew 22:36-40.

followers of Jesus Christ. Our daily "golden flecks" of service make up for the treasures of the eternities.[4]

Accumulating these precious flecks does not just happen; it takes effort and sacrifice on our part. Discipleship is the price we must pay. The apostle, Elder James E. Faust, taught:

> Everything in life has a price. Considering the Savior's great promise for peace in this life and eternal life in the life to come, discipleship is a price worth paying. It is a price we cannot afford not to pay. By measure, the requirements of discipleship are much less than the promised blessings.[5]

How do we know if we are on the pathway of discipleship? On the eve of His crucifixion, the Savior taught His apostles, "A new commandment I give unto you, That ye love one another; as I have loved you…by this shall all men know that ye are my disciples, if ye have love one to another."[6]

So what is the crowning characteristic of discipleship? It is love. It is charity. What is the motivating factor behind "[laying] up for yourselves treasures in heaven?"[7] It is love.

We ought to do the things we do day-by-day because we love God, we love our fellow men, and we respectfully love ourselves.[8]

Love and charity are interrelated but different. Charity is the deepest form of love; it is the pure love of Christ.[9] There are several aspects of charity. For example, charity is the depth of love Christ has for us, of which we need to embrace and feel.[10] In relation, we are capable of acquiring this type of love for others, and the Lord teaches how important it is that we do.

---

[4] Matthew 6:20; 3 Nephi 13:19-24; Malachi 3:2; 1 Peter 1:7.
[5] James E. Faust, "Discipleship," *Ensign*, Nov. 2006, 20-22.
[6] John 13:34-35.
[7] Matthew 6:20-21.
[8] Matthew 22:36-39.
[9] Moroni 7:43-48; 1 Corinthians 13:4; Moroni 8:17; *Doctrine and Covenants* 88:125.
[10] Ether 12:33-34; Moroni 7:47; John 15:13; *Doctrine and Covenants* 121:45.

In order to experience this deep wholesome love it takes desire, effort, and mighty prayer.[11] "Wherefore, my beloved brethren, if ye have not charity, ye are nothing, for charity never faileth. Wherefore, cleave unto charity, which is the greatest of all."[12]

The scriptures do not beat around the bush as they teach: "And except ye have charity ye can in nowise be saved in the kingdom of God; neither can ye be saved in the kingdom of God if ye have not faith; neither can ye if ye have no hope."[13] So without these three attributes—charity being the greatest—we cannot enter back into the presence of our loving Father (yikes!), which is the whole reason we are here on Earth in the first place.

The Lord does not mince words, particularly when He is talking about charity. It is essential to understand why having the gift of charity is so important in order to understand why the Service Star is necessary. This summary of 1 Corinthians 13 speaks boldly:

> And though I have the gift of prophecy, and understand all mysteries, and all knowledge; and though I have all faith, so that I could remove mountains, and have not charity, I am nothing. And though I bestow all my goods to feed the poor, and though I give my body to be burned, and have not charity, it profiteth me nothing.
>
> Charity suffereth long, and is kind; charity envieth not; charity vaunteth not itself, is not puffed up, doth not behave itself unseemly, seeketh not her own, is not easily provoked, thinketh no evil; rejoiceth not in iniquity, but rejoiceth in the truth; beareth all things, believeth all things, hopeth all things, endureth all things.
>
> Charity never faileth: but whether there be prophecies, they shall fail; whether there be tongues, they shall cease; whether there be knowledge, it shall vanish away...For

---

[11] Moroni 7:45&48; 2 Nephi 33:7-9; 2 Nephi 26:30; Colossians 3:12-14.
[12] Moroni 7:46.
[13] Moroni 10:21.

now we see through a glass, darkly; but then face to face: now I know in part; but then shall I know even as also I am known. And now abideth faith, hope, charity, these three; but the greatest of these is charity.[14]

Notice how it mentions that even if "I bestow all my goods to feed the poor," and even if I give "my body to be burned," if I "have not charity, it profiteth me nothing."[15] Wow, those seem like pretty heroic and phenomenal acts, right? Giving everything you have to the poor, and giving your body to be burned?! Sheesh, go get 'em, Tiger. Well, those are heroic acts. But sometimes an act of service itself may not always reflect the condition of the heart.[16]

Example 1

As young women, my sisters and I had been asked to participate in a service project. The request was to sew together a few blankets that would be sent to Africa. As my sisters and I worked on our creations, we noticed our little brother, Jake, observing us from the doorway in wonderment.

He approached, and then he asked in his innocent voice, "Kayla, what are you doing?" I responded, "We are making blankets for the children in Africa." He tilted his head to the side, and promptly asked, "Why?" I relayed that there were many children that did not have blankets in Africa. Jake responded with a quiet, "Oh." Then he left the room in a flash. I didn't think anything of it, and I continued casually working on the blankets.

Shortly after this conversation, my sisters and I began to pack up our blankets and walk out the front door. Suddenly, we heard a sweet child's voice cry out, "Wait!" We turned around to see Jake at the top of the stairs. He was motioning for us to follow him.

---

[14] 1 Corinthians 13:1-13.
[15] 1 Corinthians 13:3; see also Moroni 8:26.
[16] Matthew 6:1-4; 3 Nephi 13:1-4; Alma 47:32-35.

My sisters and I gave each other smiles with questioning looks as we obeyed his request. He guided us to his bedroom. As he slowly opened his bedroom door, he told us, "I made something for the children in Africa." We entered his room, and he pointed to the floor. Jake had taken about forty squares of tissue paper, and had taped them into straight rows. The tissues made a rectangular pattern that resembled a blanket. Our hearts were full of love toward our little brother. Sadly, and kindly, we relayed that we would not be able to take his tissue blanket with us. But we were deeply touched by his sincere efforts, and we assured him the Lord was pleased with him.

We thanked him again, and began to make our way back down the stairs and out the front door. We exchanged facial expressions of love and awe for Jake's condition of the heart.

As we began to make our way to the drop-off destination, my sister, Janessa, realized she had left something at the house. My sister, Ashton, and I decided to wait outside. As Janessa reentered the house, she heard a familiar child's voice say once again, "Wait!"

Janessa turned, and saw Jake motioning her towards the garage door. She promptly followed him. As Janessa made her way to the door entrance, she saw Jake holding in his little hands his *favorite* pair of shoes.

Jake looked Janessa in the eyes, and said in a pleading whisper, "If you can't give the children my blanket, will you give them my shoes?" Janessa was overwhelmed by his act of love, and her eyes began to fill up with tears. With emotion in his voice, Jake pled, "If you can't give them my shoes, I have nothing else to give."

My sisters and I have shared this story often throughout our lives. That day, we technically were the ones who did an *act of service* by sending our blankets to Africa, which was a good thing. But more than anyone, Jake was the one who portrayed the *gift of charity*.

<u>Example 2</u>

God has a pattern of sending angels to comfort His children in their hardships. When Christ took upon Himself the pains and sins of the world, He was strengthened by an angel in the Garden of Gethsemane (Bible).[17] The prophet, Alma, battled with rejection and persecution, and in the midst of these trials he was comforted by an angel (Book of Mormon).[18] You and I also have divine help from the heavens and spirit world, and we also can feel His love through the angels who are living among us.[19] Truly we are God's hands here on Earth, and the angels in our lives are doing what He would do if He were here.[20]

Medical field workers get to be a part of seeing the satisfaction of rehabilitating patients as well as the hardships of patients who are not getting better. Touching upon this subject of angels and the gift of charity, a great nursing professor of mine shared an experience with me and my classmates. It had a profound impact on me. With her permission, I now share it with you:

Hearts were heavy with unspeakable pain as a loving family was told the news that their little girl was not going to make it. Not long afterward, this little girl did indeed pass away. Her spirit entered the spirit world, and her body remained.

Words cannot describe the heaviness and sorrow that was felt. Following the little girl's death, the mother sat in the hospital room, alone, and rocked her child's little body in her arms. As she rocked her, she could not bear the thought of putting her down. She did not want one of her last memories of her precious child to be that of placing her body back in the hospital bed. Through tears, pain,

---

[17] Luke 22:42-44.
[18] Alma 8:13-15.
[19] Jeffrey R. Holland, "The Ministry of Angels," *Ensign*, Nov. 2008, 29-31; see also Alma 24:14; Alma 32:23; Hebrews 1:14; Genesis 19:15 (JST).
[20] Dieter F. Uchtdorf, "You are My Hands," *Ensign*, May 2010, 69-70, 75.

and grief, she repeatedly thought to herself, "I can't lay her down. I can't do it. I just can't lay my little girl down."

During this moment of great sorrow and perplexity, her nurse appeared at the doorway of the hospital room. The mother knew it was time to leave, and her insides churned with emotion. Through her tears, she looked at the nurse and relayed, "I'm sorry. I know she has passed away, but I just can't put her down. I can't do it."

With humility and genuine concern, the nurse looked her in the eyes and responded, "You don't have to. I will rock her for you."

With emotion and gratitude, the mother placed the little girl in the nurse's arms. That mother will never forget the sight of this nurse rocking her little girl as she left the room. Truly that nurse was sent by the Lord as an angel to this mother in this time of trial. The nurse was acting as the Lord's hands.

I cry almost every time I think of this tender experience. Taking care of paperwork and checklists are important, and may be considered *acts of service*, but those things mean nothing if we forget the reason why we are doing them. And thus it is in every individual career, relationship, and calling we may have.

This mother reflected the *gift of charity* by showing such love for her child, and this nurse also gives us an example of *Christ's charity* through the way she treated her fellowmen.

I would like to add that though this hardship still pulls on this family's heart strings, they have found hope in Christ in order to press forward. This family is sealed in the holy temple of God, and they know that they will see their little girl again (see <u>Chapter 7</u> and <u>Chapter 8</u>). The reason I know this is because the nursing instructor who shared this experience was the mother in this story. During her own nursing career, and now as a nursing instructor, she continues that nurse's legacy of charity and love among her own patients.

✹ ✹ ✹ ✹ ✹

When we are talking about charity, and God's path of eternal progression, we are not only talking about the *things we do*. God is urging us to walk the *path of becoming*. Though it may not be totally grammatically correct, in my heart and mind I like to think of this process as "becoming charity." Charity is something we have, and it is something of our character. It is not only the things we do, it is a gift from the Lord.

In my teenage years, I was praying to know what the Lord would have me do at my school in order to be a light unto others. At that time, I was reading in the book of Alma. When I came to Alma 37:6, I had an unexpected experience.

Alma 37:6 teaches: "By small and simple things are great things brought to pass."

This simple scriptural verse "seemed to enter with great force into every feeling of my heart…I reflected on it again and again."[21] I have quoted Alma 37:6 many times already in this book. This passage is so basic, and it truly has changed my life.

I realized that I did not need to do anything grand in order to make a difference at my school. All I needed to do was focus on "small and simple" acts of kindness toward others.

I was reminded that diligent, sincere, Christ-like gestures in our day-to-day interactions with others truly bring about "great things." These simple deeds will accumulate over time into new friendships, quality relationships, healed hearts, smiles, laughs, and even subtle yet significant miracles.[22] Those are great things. Striving to become charity is a great thing, and eternal life is a great thing. And how do we get there? We arrive one step at time through our daily choices.

Alma 37:6 can apply to a multitude of things, and it continues to be a guide in my life. I have a long way to go, but thankfully we

---

[21] *Joseph Smith-History* 1:12.
[22] *Doctrine and Covenants* 123:16-17.

"become charity" one day at time as we apply Christ's Atonement and serve others as His disciples. This is attainable and valuable.

The Goal of the Service Star

The goal of the Service Star is to do an act of kindness for someone every day. The Service Star is not another checklist item on our grocery list. The goal is to *do* something for someone daily, but the essence of this goal is that we are motivated to *become* a little more like the Savior in our day-to-day interactions.

You and I are to strive to be walking, talking, beacons of light.[23] We can reflect in our own lives the grand compliment given to the Savior as One "who went about doing good."[24] He is phenomenal. He will help us in the process of becoming more like Him.

Again, the condition of our hearts as we "go about doing good" is the true reflection of becoming charity. Service should not be given to "be seen [by others]" or to show off how charitable we are.[25] Jesus taught, "Let not thy left hand know what thy right hand doeth."[26] He set the flawless example of this. When Jesus would help someone, He would regularly instruct them not to tell anyone, and I find it significant that His disciples wrote: "And there are also many other things which Jesus did, the which, if they should be written every one, I suppose that even the world itself could not contain the books that should be written."[27] Wow. Jesus is the King of personal, thoughtful, anonymous service.

We read account after account in the scriptures of Christ giving genuine service to those who were sick, lonely, heart broken, cruelly judged, stricken with the guilt of sin, hopeless, tired, and sad.[28] His

---

[23] Matthew 5:14-16; 3 Nephi 18:24.
[24] Acts 10:38.
[25] Matthew 6:1-4; Alma 26:11-12.
[26] Matthew 6:3.
[27] John 21:24-25; see also Matthew 8:2-4; Mark 7:36; Luke 8:43-48; Matthew 9:27-30; Luke 8:49-56.
[28] John 8:2-11; Mark 5:22-43; John 9:1-11; Mormon 1:15; Alma 7:11; John 11:32-35; Mosiah 3:7; Luke 18:15-17; Matthew 4:23-24; Mark 6:34-44; Psalm 147:3; Alma 15:8; 3 Nephi 17:8-9; Luke 17:11-19.

atoning sacrifice was the ultimate act of service ever given. The Service Star allows for continued application of Christ's atoning power in our lives and helps us to become like Him.[29]

The "How" of the Service Star

We have learned about what the Service Star is and why it is so important, now let's talk about the how. In order to achieve the Service Star, the most helpful action is to follow the challenge of Elder M. Russell Ballard. His inspired challenge was to "pray every morning to find someone to serve" and then to "stay focused."[30]

Acts of goodness are going to vary from day-to-day. One day, it may be a simple text to someone on your mind containing a scripture and the words: "I was thinking of you, I sure love ya!" Another day, it may be taking the time to help someone in the grocery line who has their hands full. Some other possibilities for our Service Star can include: giving a heartfelt compliment, reminding someone that God loves them, making dinner for a roommate, visiting a nursing home, writing a sincere letter to a loved one, or spending special one-on-one time with a child who seems to be struggling.

Genuine service can be as simple as making a sack lunch for a spouse, tucking a child into bed, sitting by someone seated alone at church, or holding the door open. Thoughtfulness matters.

These simple "drops" of kindness make a "ripple effect" of a positive difference in this world. If we are doing these things with a sincere heart and with an attitude of charity, we will be on our way to seeing more as the Savior sees, and truly "taking His name upon us."[31] I have noticed that individuals who choose to "first observe, then serve" seem to have a special glow in their countenances; it

---

[29] M. Russell Ballard, "Finding Joy Through Loving Service," *Ensign*, May 2011, 46-48.
[30] M. Russell Ballard, "Be Anxiously Engaged," *Ensign*, Nov. 2012, 29.
[31] Moroni 4:3; *Doctrine and Covenants* 20:77; Alma 46:18.

seems to be a reflection of that Being whom they are striving to emulate.[32]

Two important service opportunities include paying tithing and fast offerings. Tithing is a commandment from God to give ten percent of our annual earnings to help build His kingdom here on the earth (temples, church buildings, missionary work, etc.).[33] The immense blessings we can receive from exercising the faith to pay tithing are remarkable.[34] Paying tithing is a blessing.

Also, one Sunday per month is set aside for the opportunity to fast. This day is often referred to as Fast Sunday. On this day we have the privilege of giving a personal donation of money to help the poor and the needy in our local communities (this donation is called a fast offering).[35] This is a wonderful service opportunity. I know from personal experience that when we trust in God and follow the admonition to make tithing and fast offering financial priorities, our financial needs are met.

The Lord's church is organized in such a way that we can help each other in many ways. As a congregation, we call each other "brother" and "sister." This can act as a reminder of our need to take care of each other. An important way to watch after each other is through home teaching and visiting teaching. Each member of the local congregation is routinely assigned home teachers (two male priesthood holders) and visiting teachers (two females) that visit at least once a month to befriend, teach, and serve that individual or family. Home and visiting teaching should be our Service Star of the day often. My eldest brother, Jason, has always been a stalwart home teacher throughout every phase of his busy life. Even while he was

[32] Linda K. Burton, "First Observe, Then Serve," *Ensign*, Nov. 2012, 78-80; see Alma 5:14&19.
[33] David A. Bednar, "The Windows of Heaven," *Ensign*, Nov. 2013, 17-20; see Malachi 3:10; Genesis 14:19-20; *Doctrine and Covenants* 59:12-16; Hebrews 7:2; *Doctrine and Covenants* 119:4; 3 Nephi 24:8-11.
[34] Robert D. Hales, "Tithing: A Test of Faith with Eternal Blessings," *Ensign*, Nov. 2002, *lds.org*, The Church of Jesus Christ of Latter-day Saints, Nov. 2002 (accessed June 7, 2017); see Malachi 3:10.
[35] Joseph B. Wirthlin, "The Law of the Fast," *Ensign*, May 2001, *lds.org* (accessed June 9, 2017); see Deuteronomy 15:11; Isaiah 58:6-12; Malachi 3:8-12; Alma 34:28; Alma 6:6.

in the trenches of dental school, with the added responsibilities of being a husband and a dad of young kids, he continued to magnify his callings. He must have learned well from the example of Christ and other positive role models to "feed [His] sheep," to "succor the weak," to "lift up the hands which hang low," and to "strengthen the feeble knees."[36] The Lord extends this call to all.

I know, through personal experience, that the Lord will answer our prayers to find someone to serve. This is a subtle miracle we need daily. We may not always know why we have a feeling to reach out to a certain person, but the Lord knows who needs us every day. Here are several helpful examples.

Example 1

My sister, Ashton, had taken on the service challenge from Elder Ballard. One day, she gave her usual supplication to be guided to someone she could help. She then went about her daily tasks, and she stayed focused. Subtly throughout the day she had the thought to call a certain elderly lady she had met at church. Ashton hardly knew her, but the feeling persisted. She heeded the prompting, and awkwardly picked up the phone and dialed the lady's number.

While she listened to the stagnant ringing, she thought to herself, "Uhhh what am I going to say?!" Ashton said a silent prayer in her heart, and waited until she heard a voice on the other end of the line. Her heart rate increased as she heard, "Hello?" Ashton took a deep breath, and chose to follow through with the prompting she had received from the Spirit. She began, "Hey! This is Ashton from church, I have been thinking of you today, and thought I would call you."

The lady's voice got quiet on the other end, and she whispered, "You thought to call me?"

---

[36] John 21:17; Mosiah 23:18; *Doctrine and Covenants* 81:5; Isaiah 35:3; Mosiah 4:16.

Ashton responded with a simple, "Ya! How are you today?" A few seconds of silence followed, and then the lady replied with emotion in her voice, "How did you know it was my birthday?"

This elderly sister spent many days alone, and she was touched beyond words that someone remembered her on this special day.

Ashton did not know it was her birthday, but God did. Ashton's heart filled with gratitude for the Lord's awareness of this sweet old lady and of each of us. He is involved in the very details of our lives.

It would have been so easy for Ashton to make excuses like: "I do not even know her, how awkward," or "I am not assigned to visit teach her; what could I even do to help?" Ashton was an example of the process of discipleship, and charity, by following through with her prompting after having prayed to the Father to find someone to serve that day. *Do something for someone every day!*

A touching parallel was shared in the Sunday program Music and the Spoken Word:

> For many years now, one woman has made it her practice to start her day by thinking about who might need her help. Who can she call? Who can she visit? Who might need a little sunshine? Somehow she can always think of someone; there's no shortage of people to reach out to. Sometimes she offers nothing more than a listening ear; other times she brings small gifts or food, but she gives a portion of herself—only to have it replenished for the next day's giving!
>
> Yes, there's certainly a lot to complain about in life. But giving of ourselves not only shifts our focus away from our problems, it also allows us to make the world just a little more beautiful—even if it's only in small ways. As the university leader wisely observed, "Generally speaking, the most miserable people I know are those who are

obsessed with themselves; the happiest people I know are those who lose themselves in the service of others."[37]

I have a personal testimony that the Lord knows who needs our help each day, and we are happiest when we choose to serve daily. *Do something for someone every day!*

Example 2

Another example can be seen in an experience I had while I was serving as a missionary in Argentina. I had only been on the mission for a small amount of time, and I was with my first companion (my "trainer"). For me, understanding and being understood in the Spanish language took diligence and patience. However, despite the communication barrier at the beginning of the mission, I still felt an immense love for the people of Argentina.

One day, my trainer and I had baked some banana bread and we prayed to the Lord to know if there was anyone in particular that could use the loaf. A particular elderly lady we knew came to our minds as someone who could benefit from receiving the loaf of bread. We got ready to go to bed, and we planned to visit her that next evening before we came home. That would be an obvious and convenient plan. Well, the Lord had other plans.

We woke up at 6:30 am to exercise, and I knelt at my bedside to pray. As I began to communicate with my Heavenly Father, I had this feeling that we needed to give the elderly lady her banana bread *right now*. I recall saying in my mind, "Uh, right now?" The thought came again, subtle yet constant, that we needed to give her the loaf immediately. I ended my prayer, put on my running shoes, and grabbed the banana bread.

I awkwardly walked over to my trainer, and said, "Umm...sister, this is kind of odd and random, but I have a feeling that we need to

---

[37] *Music and the Spoken Word*, May 22, 2016 - #4523, *mormontabernaclechoir.org* (accessed May 19, 2016).

deliver this bread right now." My trainer looked at me, and said, "Well, it is 6 am in the morning, you really mean like right now?"

I briefly paused, and then replied, "It's weird, but yes." My great trainer responded with words of faith, "Alright, let's go." With the loaf of banana bread in hand, we took off running into the early morning darkness. We typically met with this lady at church, so we had only been to her house a handful of times.

Have fun imagining this early morning scene in slow-motion (dramatic music in the background is acceptable): There we were, two determined sister missionaries, banana bread in hand, running through the mists of dawn to give an elderly lady a loaf bread.

Why? Because the Lord asked us to.

Through the pure guidance of the Spirit, my trainer was able to lead us to the lady's house in the morning blackness. Amazing!

Her home was located in the very back of a group of houses that were closed off by a railed gate. As we arrived at the gate, we did not know how we could possibly get the bread to her doorstep. Without getting through the gate it was a lost cause. Now isn't that just devastating?! So close, yet so far.

We just stood there for a moment in silence. Then suddenly, we noticed movement outside one of the houses located nearest to the gate. That specific neighbor "just so happened" to be awake at 6 am letting his dogs out. I think we kind of startled him. Bless his soul. For our cause, it was a true miracle.

We kindly asked him to place the bread loaf on the appropriate doormat. Then we ran home, partially laughing in wonderment. We felt joy and contentment in our hearts, even though we did not know why we needed to do this unusual task.

Later that week we saw that elderly lady at church. She came up to me, and said, "I know the bread on my doormat was from you two." In my broken Spanish, I tried to act bewildered—but did not want to lie—so I asked her how she knew.

She relayed that she had been visiting an ill family member and had gotten home late the night before. Because of her late arrival to her house she was unable to make food to eat for work the next day. She woke up early the next morning for work, with discouragement and a heavy heart. Remembering that she was not going to be able to eat all day, she prayed to the Lord for strength.

As she headed out the door, she saw the banana bread placed on her doorstep. With bread in hand, she walked to work in the early morning darkness. She was emotional because she knew the loaf was sent from the Lord.

I know God was aware of her, and for our benefit and joy, He sent us to be His hands. May we always answer His calls. Subtle yet significant miracles happen when we serve the Lord and follow His promptings. *Do something for someone every day!*

Example 3

This touching experience shared by President Dieter F. Uchtdorf has inspired me many times. This story is about the beloved prophet Thomas S. Monson. President Uchtdorf related the experience:

> I would like to say a few words about President Thomas S. Monson. Some years ago, President Monson came to a regional conference in Hamburg, Germany, and it was my honor to accompany him. President Monson has a remarkable memory, and we talked about many of the Saints in Germany—I was amazed that he remembered so many so well.
>
> President Monson asked about Michael Panitsch, a former stake president and then a patriarch, who had been one of the stalwart pioneers of the Church in Germany. I told him that Brother Panitsch was seriously ill, that he was bedridden and unable to attend our meetings.
>
> President Monson asked if we could pay him a visit. I knew that shortly before his trip to Hamburg, President

Monson had undergone foot surgery and that he could not walk without pain. I explained that Brother Panitsch lived on the fifth floor of a building with no elevators. We would have to climb the stairs to see him.

But President Monson insisted. And so we went.

I remember how difficult it was for President Monson to climb those stairs. He could take only a few at a time before needing to stop and rest. He never uttered a word of complaint, and he would not turn back. Because the building had high ceilings, the stairs seemed to go on forever, but President Monson cheerfully persevered until we arrived at the apartment of Brother Panitsch on the fifth floor.

Once there, we had a wonderful visit. President Monson thanked him for his life of dedicated service and cheered him with a smile. Before we left, he gave him a wonderful priesthood blessing. No one but Brother Panitsch, the immediate family, and myself ever saw that act of courage and compassion.

President Monson could have chosen to rest between our long and frequent meetings. He could have asked to see some of the beautiful sights of Hamburg. I have often thought of how remarkable it was that of all the sights in that city, the one he wanted to see more than any other was a feeble and ailing member of the Church who had faithfully and humbly served the Lord.

President Monson came to Hamburg to teach and bless the people of a country, and that is what he did. But at the same time, he focused on the one, name by name.[38]

It makes sense why President Thomas S. Monson has taught so often, "A friendly smile, a warm handclasp, a sincere testimony of

---

[38] Dieter F. Uchtdorf, "Faith of Our Father," *Ensign*, May 2008, 68-75.

truth can literally lift lives, change human nature, and save precious souls."[39] He knows from experience. *Do something for someone every day!*

Example 4

A young gal in my sister's young women's class shared a tender experience. Her six-year-old brother is blind and loves to pretend that the closet is an elevator. He makes the sound effects of pushing buttons and moving people up or down to the floor they need to get to. He wants to play again, and again, and again, and it can get old. Then one day, the young woman realized that using his imagination is the only way her brother can "see" the world. This perspective resulted in enhanced compassion within her. She can now play with her brother without feeling annoyed. *Do something for someone every day!*

Example 5

I was not planning on sharing this example, but it was repeatedly brought up by many people to be something significant to share. So, may we all apply this to ourselves in our individual circumstances. This experience also took place while I was serving as a full-time missionary in Argentina.

My companion and I had one of those days in which we walked a lot—like a strenuous more than usual type of "a lot." Those days can happen every now and then. It is tempting to feel discouraged. However, those types of experiences can bring about subtle miracles as well. We just need to keep moving forward, and make an effort to recognize the good in the day. In a nutshell, days like that bring sure growth to our souls—reflecting to ourselves and the Lord that we are willing to do things He wants us to do no matter what. As we strode onward, we silently prayed along our way.

After the continuous cycle of failed plans and rejection, we felt impressed to stop by a certain church member's house. This sister

---

[39] Thomas S. Monson, "To Learn, to Do, to Be," *Ensign*, Nov. 2008, 62.

meant a lot to us, and we had become great friends. She had begun attending church regularly for the first time in years. She admitted that she had always desired to return, but Satan's lies kept her away.

We arrived to her doorstep and knocked on the door. We were unexpectedly greeted by the tear-streaked face of this dear sister. She let us in, without words. Then she fell on the couch sobbing in the fetal position. My companion and I looked at each other for a moment, unsure of what to do. We stooped down to the level of the couch and gently asked her what was wrong. She began to tearfully disclose that she was having family conflicts, and on top of that, felt like no one in the world cared about her. We felt to say nothing; we extended a hand for strength, and she grabbed on lifting her weary body to the standing position. She was then wrapped in an embrace and allowed to cry.

With time, wails turned to whimpers and sobs turned to sniffles. I stepped back, looked her in the eyes, and from the depths of my soul confirmed to her that she was loved and needed by the people around her. More than anything, the Lord loved her and was clearly aware of her. I testified that God had sent us to remind her of those truths. She mattered to God.

That night, as we returned to our apartment, we prayed to know how to help this sister become the woman the Lord intended her to become. The answer that came to us was: "Teach her how to serve."

The next day, we arranged a visit with her with the mandate and goal to get her out of the house to meet her neighbors. We made cookies and put them on a little plate. We arrived to her house and told her the plan. As we knelt with her in prayer, she lifted up a sincere plea to the Lord to be guided. She closed the prayer with the statement, "The missionaries have told me that if I serve I will feel a lot better, and I will understand my purpose. Help me to know if this is true. Help us to be a blessing in the lives of my neighbors…"

We then left to visit a neighbor she felt we should see. We had a wonderful visit with that neighbor, and they were grateful for and surprised at the kind gesture of us bringing cookies just because. We gathered in their home, conversing about life and of Christ. It was wonderful. When we left, we saw a greater brightness in the face of the neighbor, and we felt greater joy within ourselves.

We then reloaded the plate with more cookies and made our way to the next neighbor she felt we should visit. This exchange was shorter, but the effects were the same.

As we walked our friend back to her home, I can sincerely say I had never seen her so happy. In her face, I did not see hopelessness anymore. There was a light. I saw more of the Savior in her. For truly His light was in there all along.[40]

Over the several months that I was in that area, I saw a growth in that sister that was a heavenly result of striving to do what she could. She began to choose to be the one to sit by those sitting alone at church. She would choose to go out to visit those in need more often. She became one of the go-to service members and befrienders to those who did not have friends. *Do something for someone every day!*

Example 6

My brother, Zach, served a faithful mission in Mexico, and he is still a great example of service. He often helps around the house without being told and he is fun to be around. One week, he wrote home these wonderful insights:

I've seen that so many times in the mission we will say a prayer for guidance in the morning, and then we will just be walking and have a thought to visit someone. It's just like, "Yeah why not? Let's go visit that individual." When we show up, almost always that individual is struggling with something, and we

---

[40] Alma 5:14; Matthew 6:22.

came just in time. That is something about service that I've learned. We are all in the same process of learning and progressing.

If we have the thought to reach out to someone and we just think, "Oh that individual is coming to church every week so everything is great!"…we are wrong. So many people are just waiting for a visit or a hug. We are all in this work together. As Christ teaches in the parable of the lost sheep, we are to seek after that LOST 1 or a completely NEW sheep to bring to the fold.[41] *However, we can't forget about the 99 that are right by our side, maybe on the edge of wandering off! 100 is our goal!*

I love these insights from Zach. I think it is so easy to dismiss a thought to reach out to someone or to doubt our ability to receive personal revelation. It is of utmost importance that we learn how to trust and understand this divine direction from God. *Do something for someone every day!*

Understanding and Finding Joy in Promptings

At times it can be tempting to deny the guidance of the Lord and second-guess ourselves. Wouldn't it be nice to have a formula to know if I am receiving a prompting from the Lord or if I am having a thought that is "just coming from me?" Well, we do indeed have the formula!

Moroni 7:16 teaches: "I show unto you the way to judge; for everything which inviteth to do good, and to persuade to believe in Christ, is sent forth by the power and gift of Christ; wherefore ye may know with a perfect knowledge it is of God."[42]

In a nut shell, if we have the thought to do something good, we need to do it! I like this supporting scripture in the Doctrine and Covenants: "And now, verily, verily, I say unto thee, put your trust

---

[41] Luke 15:4-5.
[42] Moroni 7:16.

in that Spirit which leadeth to do good—yea, to do justly, to walk humbly, to judge righteously; and this is my Spirit."[43]

When we receive a prompting, may we always keep in mind the command to "preach the gospel to every creature" through simple acts of invitation and service on behalf of those around us.[44] The more we act upon the impressions of the Spirit, the more the voice of the Spirit becomes familiar to us. This demonstrates to the Lord that He can trust us with any assignment from Him. The more we practice, the easier it gets. The prophet Thomas S. Monson taught:

> The sweetest experience I know in life is to feel a prompting and act upon it and later find out that it was the fulfillment of someone's prayer or someone's need. And I always want the Lord to know that if He needs an errand run, Tom Monson will run that errand for Him.[45]

We will find ourselves in situations in which we are called to do things that are more time demanding than sending a text. There may be days when we have the feeling to stop by someone's house and come to find they needed a good two hour chat. The Lord needed us to be the angel sent on His behalf. Experiences will come where we may feel to stop and help someone with a flat tire, or accompany an individual who is sick at the hospital.

Sometimes, we are called to do things that could be considered outside of our comfort zone or even inconvenient, but when the Lord calls we can heed knowing He will sustain us.[46] Among one of the most powerful phrases in all scripture is the response, "Here am I, send me."[47] President Dieter F. Uchtdorf taught:

---

[43] *Doctrine and Covenants* 11:12.
[44] Mark 16:15; Mosiah 28:3; *Doctrine and Covenants* 58:64.
[45] "Messages of Inspiration from President Monson," *Church News*, Sept. 2, 2012, 2.
[46] David A. Bednar, "In the Strength of the Lord," Oct.2001, *speeches.byu.edu* (accessed May 5, 2016).
[47] Isaiah 6:8; 2 Nephi 16:8; 1 Nephi 3:7.

Often, the answer to our prayer does not come while we're on our knees but while we're on our feet serving the Lord and serving those around us. Selfless acts of service and consecration refine our spirits, remove the scales from our spiritual eyes, and open the windows of heaven. By becoming the answer to someone's prayer, we often find the answer to our own.[48]

It is important to remember that not every service opportunity is going to be received with gratitude. That cannot deter us in the pathway of discipleship and charity. Press on with hope!

Often we may be quick to judge our ability to get along with another person. Follow the promptings of the Lord and have the courage to be kind.

All of my family members have been good examples to me of service. This includes my youngest brother, Jake, who I shared a story about earlier. During Jake's high school student government retreat, he taught his peers of the importance of being kind to all genres of people at school. During Jake's lesson, one of the class officers was sitting by the head cheerleader. The cheerleader had severely hurt her ankle at cheer practice a few days prior and was confined to using crutches. They all had to help her at times during the day with the activities they were doing.

At the end of the retreat, that particular class officer relayed that she had always hated cheerleaders and did not want anything to do with them. After being together all day, and taking time to serve this cheerleader, she gained a new attitude. She was even caught carrying the cheerleader on her back—helping her across two roads—as the group made their way to their destination. I wish that everyone at their high school could have been at this special retreat and felt the walls of judgement go down and the bonds of friendship made.

---

[48] Dieter F. Uchtdorf, "Waiting on the Road to Damascus," *Ensign*, May 2011, 70-72.

Serving at Your Phase of Life

Something important to note is that we are all in our own phases of life. Each era brings particular opportunities to serve. We ought to be grateful for each stage of service that comes with each new chapter of our lives. We will have the capacity to serve in ways today that will be different than the opportunities that may come in ten years. Remember that the Lord "looketh upon the heart."[49] He does want us to give what we can with our current circumstances, but He does not want us to "run faster than we have strength."[50]

Keep in mind that the scriptures teach us to "succor those who stand in need of *your* succor"[51] There are people that need *you*— yes, specifically you—to be the Lord's angel sent to befriend, uplift, and comfort them. No matter what phase of life you are in, strive to feel the spirit of the Service Star by living your life in such a way that people feel safe, uplifted, and loved in *your* presence. *Do something for someone every day!*

Our Families Deserve Our Best Service

When we are talking about the Service Star, remember that our families are the ones who should receive our A-game service. Have you ever fallen prey to being more kind to strangers than to your own family? Boo! I know I have. Satan loves it when we do this! Argh, he is so annoying!

Jesus Christ continually gave His best efforts to His family. Even to the extent that one of His last phrases uttered in mortality and one of his last requests while on the cross—the Son of God in excruciating pain and agony—was to have John care for His Mom.

---

49 1 Samuel 16:7.
50 Mosiah 4:27.
51 Mosiah 4:16; emphasis added.

"When Jesus therefore saw his mother, and the disciple standing by, whom he loved, he saith unto his mother, Woman, behold thy son! Then saith he to the disciple, Behold thy mother! And from that hour that disciple took her unto his own home."[52]

President Uchtdorf taught, "Families are not just meant to make things run more smoothly here on Earth and to be cast off when we get to heaven. Rather, they are the order of heaven. They are an echo of a celestial pattern and an emulation of God's eternal family."[53]

The family is a unit of teamwork, and is the most sacred place to "practice." Though women do not hold the priesthood, they have divine capabilities that play a vital part in the Lord's holy order that are no more or less necessary than the role of men.[54]

In the Lord's order, the father holds a divine gift that helps him guide his family and serve others. This gift is the priesthood that he holds. The mother holds the unique and divine power of being able to give birth to children. Serving and lifting others is a part of her divine nature. This is one of God's unchanging patterns.[55]

The prophet David O. McKay taught, "The home is the basis of a righteous life, and no other instrumentality can take its place, nor fulfill its essential functions."[56] Elder Neal A. Maxwell added:

> There are no perfect families, either in the world or in the Church, but there are many good families. My spiritual applause also goes to those heroic parents—left alone by death or divorce—who are righteously and "anxiously engaged" in nurturing and providing for their families.[57]

---

52 John 19:26-27.
53 Dieter F. Uchtdorf, "In Praise of Those Who Save," *Ensign*, May 2016, 77-80; "The Family: A Proclamation to the World," *lds.org* (accessed May 19, 2016).
54 1 Corinthians 11:11; Acts 9:36-40; Alma 56:47-48; Romans 16:1-2; *Doctrine and Covenants* 25:1; Proverbs 31:10; "The Family: A Proclamation to the World," *lds.org* (accessed May 1, 2016); *Bible Dictionary:* Temple.
55 Dallin H. Oaks, "The Keys and Authority of the Priesthood," *Ensign*, May 2014, 49-52; "The Family: A Proclamation to the World," *lds.org* (accessed April 20, 2017).
56 *Family Home Evening Manual* (The Church of Jesus Christ of Latter-day Saints, 1965), preface.
57 Neal A. Maxwell, "Take Especial Care of Your Family," *Ensign*, May 1994, *lds.org*, (accessed April 19, 2017).

If you do not have a worthwhile family situation at present, have peace in the promises of the Lord that "all things work together for good [for those] that love God."[58] Thomas S. Monson taught, "Let us...find joy in the journey and share our love with friends and family. Let us not put off what is most important."[59]

Example 1

When my mom and dad were first married, my mom was asked to help take dinner to a family that had just had a new baby. She was more than willing to help, and she put together a delicious salad. The salad was left sitting in the fridge, ready to go. When my dad came home from work, he looked in the fridge and was so excited to see a delicious salad waiting for him. Just as he was pulling the salad out of the fridge, my mom had to politely tell him that it was not for him, it was for the neighbors.

She paused for a moment and then realized that it was pretty sad for her to admit that this yummy salad was not for her sweetheart. She learned a great lesson that day: we should always strive to give our best efforts to our families first, and then reach out to serve others from there. Now, whenever she is called to make dinner for other people, she always makes enough to feed her own family too. She is a humble, faithful servant of the Lord.

Example 2

Here is another important story involving my mom. I have been floored by my mom and dad's ability to care for our family. One day, I asked my mom what prompted her to put family first. She said she had many positive examples in her life. One grand example was her mother-in-law (my grandma).

---

58 Romans 8:28; *Doctrine and Covenants* 90:24.
59 Thomas S. Monson, "Love At Home-Counsel from a Prophet," *Ensign*, Aug. 2011, *lds.org*, The Church of Jesus Christ of Latter-day Saints, August 2011 (accessed January 6, 2017).

My mom relayed that, while she was dating my dad, he trained for and ran a 10k race. Like a super awesome girlfriend, she went to support him. Afterward, they stopped by my dad's house to eat some breakfast.

My dad asked my mom if she wanted some cereal. She accepted the invitation, and my dad went to the kitchen cupboard and pulled out some fine china bowls for them to eat their cereal in. My mom was confused as to why they would use the fine china for a bowl of cereal. She whispered, "Uh...are we really allowed to use these?" My dad looked at her, and obliviously replied, "Well ya, it's what we always use." She ate her cereal in awe.

As she continued to date my dad, and eventually married him, she took note of other things. She observed a helpful attitude and love expressed among all the members of his large family (woot woot ten siblings!). She also noticed that the punch bowl was used any day, not just special occasions. In time, my mom resolved to ask my grandma about all these observations, especially the china bowls.

When my mom inquired about these things, my grandma looked her in the eyes, and humbly answered, "I received that fine china at my wedding. I decided that very day that instead of putting it on a shelf, or in a box to be preserved, I was going to use it often with the people that I loved most. For isn't every day a special occasion?"

My mom learned from the grand example of my grandma—and many righteous relatives—that our families are worth "bringing out the fine china," or rather, giving our best effort.

Important Reminder

As a general review, the Service Star is so much more than just checking off a list and saying, "I did something for someone, check! I'm awesome." Although doing something for someone is the goal, remember that the Service Star is so much more about following the

Savior's example. This Star assists us in the pathway of discipleship, the journey of acquiring the gift of charity, and acting upon the promptings of the Lord. This changes everything. Elder M. Russell Ballard reminded us:

> [I don't] suggest that our challenges today are more severe than the challenges faced by those who have gone before us. They are just different. The Lord isn't asking us to load up a handcart; He's asking us to fortify our faith. He isn't asking us to walk across a continent; He's asking us to walk across the street to visit our neighbor. He isn't asking us to die a martyr's death; He's asking us to live a disciple's life.[60]

As we strive to become a walking, talking Service Star, our true and genuine interactions with others will change lives. The vitality of this Star (with the effects on our personal happiness) can only be experienced by taking this challenge seriously. God lives to help and guide His children; may we show Him our gratitude by loving and helping each other. Truly, He lives to serve us; may we live to serve Him.[61]

It is important to serve others as well as take time to personally reconnect with heaven. That leads us to our next Star!

[60] M. Russell Ballard, "The Truth of God Shall Go Forth," *Ensign*, Nov. 2008, 81-84.
[61] Moses 1:39; Romans 5:8; 2 Nephi 26:24; Psalm 86:15.

Chapter 7

5 Star Day:

Sacred Time

THE DICTIONARY IS filled with hundreds of thousands of words. In all their varieties, each word has a unique meaning. Some words may take on a deeper, more personal, significance to us than others.

During the blessed hour of elementary school library time, my friends and I used to grab the huge dictionary at the back of the room on the prized pedestal, and we would play a game. We would begin by talking about some superficial subject and then, midway through the conversation, we would fling the book open to some obscure page and dramatically point to any word. The word pointed at had to be instantly implemented into the conversation. We would do this repeatedly, and it made for a good laugh as well as a frequently "shush"-ing librarian. Unusual words were appreciated by us. There were so many I could not remember them all if I tried.

What do you think would be the most important word in the dictionary? I feel there are words that can be considered collectively among the most valuable. A few of these words may include: love, loyalty, charity, atone, forgive, resurrect, heal, endure, believe, faith, hope, etc. Another significant word is discussed by the prophet Spencer W. Kimball:

> When you look in the dictionary for the most important word, do you know what it is? It could be *"remember."* Because all of [us] have made covenants…our greatest need is to *remember.* That is why everyone goes to sacrament meeting every Sabbath day—to take the sacrament and listen to the priests pray that [we] "may always *remember* him and keep his commandments which he has given [us]."…*"Remember"* is the word.[1]

This word has had a positive impact on my life and the Sacred Time Star is founded upon it. Remember.

The Purpose of the Sacred Time Star

Ashton, Janessa, and Jacoby (my cousin) had great insights for the initial groundwork of the Sacred Time Star. This Star used to be called the Sacred Grove or Self Reflection Star. These two indicators are still wonderful and valid descriptors, and they have helped us get to where we are today. With time and guidance, God assisted us in understanding that choosing to *reconnect with heaven* and *Remember* is the focus of this important Star.

We live in a world that is loud and busy. There is great benefit in slowing down for a moment and getting away from the noise. My sister, Ashton, calls this "reconnecting with heaven." I love this phrase. This phrase is utilized not to infer that you are not already connected with heaven or that the other Stars in this book are not connecting you with heaven. Rather, I use this phrase to remind you that the Sacred Time Star is a separate act and conscious decision to

---

[1] Spencer W. Kimball, "Circles of Exaltation" (address to religious educators, Brigham Young University, 28 June 1968), 8.

slow down away from worldly noise. It can be physically, mentally, emotionally, and spiritually empowering to take time to refocus and Remember.

It was not until my teenage years that I even began to scratch the surface of the deep significance of the word "remember." The summer after my high school graduation, I went on a church history tour where I visited places where significant spiritual events had taken place in the life of Joseph Smith and the early saints of Christ's restored church. Since that tour, the teachings that magnify the deep meaning of the word "remember" have been engrained upon my soul.

Thus, it is with great respect that I choose to capitalize the word Remember when referring to it in this sacred way. Later on in this chapter, I will relate some significant experiences I had while traveling on this church history tour.

It is helpful that the first several sections of this chapter address the teachings related to the gift of Remembrance and what that even means. From there, we will be able to dive into learning about two crucial holy places that can facilitate reconnection with heaven and Remembrance. For the finale, we will learn about daily opportunities to instigate the Sacred Time Star. You will come to find that all parts of this chapter are distinct yet interrelated in a significant way.

I encourage you to pay particular attention to the way you feel as you read the upcoming sections teaching about the word *Remember.* Ponder about what you are learning and how it may translate into your own life. The understanding and application of these teachings, and how they apply to your personal life, have the potential to change everything. *Remember* is the "why" of the Sacred Time Star, and it is the "why" of crucial concepts of Christ's gospel.

Remember

There was a time in my life when I had the blessing to work as a home health nurse. The patients that were in my care were stable enough that they did not need to be in the hospital, but were critical to the point that they always needed trained individuals with them.

All of my patients struggled with complex congenital diseases. These disease processes eventually led them to not being able to get out of bed. Also, ventilator machines breathed on their behalf, and tubes were inserted straight into their stomachs to allow nutrition to enter their bodies. I was in their homes for up to ten hours per day.

There was one middle-aged patient in particular that I took care of more regularly than the others. When working with this patient, I was allowed to read a book of my choice whenever he slept. I chose to read the scriptures. With time, he began to take note of this.

One day, he opened up to me about the hefty trials he had been through in his lifetime. Bullies and religious hypocrites had caused him much harm in his childhood and teenage years. He expressed, "I used to believe in God, but now I am not so sure." Gently, I validated his concerns. I promised him that he could come to know if God is real by experimenting upon His word.

After months of getting to know each other, he began to request that I read the scriptures to him. When he first asked, I played it way cool with a nonchalant, "Sure." Inside I was hootin' and hollerin' internal celebrations (see Chapter 4 if you need a reminder of the incredible blessings that flow into our lives when we choose to read the scriptures daily)! Woot Woot!

I would hold up his different options and ask which he wanted to read. At the beginning, he chose to read in the Bible. He would typically choose the books with the most unique names, and that made me smile. One casual day he asked to read in Deuteronomy.

Chapter 1 in Deuteronomy teaches that the Israelites—except Caleb and Joshua—were not living worthy of entering the promised land (i.e. the land the Lord had prepared for them and guided them to).[2] The children of Israel complained that God led them out of Egypt just to destroy them.[3] Let me tell you, it is quite frustrating to read about these choice people choosing to forget the Lord and His guidance. It makes you want to say, "Get a grip people! Live worthy of the promised land!"

In previous chapters, the Lord delivered them from slavery (and in the process protected them with a pillar of fire), and God parted the Red Sea for them to cross.[4] Once they were free, the Lord had been raining manna (a bread-like meal) on them for daily sustenance according to their needs.[5] He also led them by a cloud during the day and a pillar of fire at night.[6] Wow! How incredible is the Lord?!

Traveling through the wilderness is not easy, but God provided the way. Sadly, the Israelites did not appreciate the miracles around them. An alarming reality about this is that the children of Israel are a symbolic type of all of God's children. That includes you and me. Are we really that blind to the incredible miracles and the hand of the Lord in our own lives?

My patient was saddened by the Israelites' lack of faith, and he asked, "How could the children of Israel be like that when it was so evident that the Lord was in their lives?"

I pondered on this for a moment. Remembrance filled my soul, and I responded, "I was given the answer to that question during a life-changing church history tour the summer after high school."

I explained to my patient the restoration of Christ's gospel, and the significance of the tour (in that we were blessed to visit sacred locations of some of the critical events that took place in the process of this restoration; see Chapter 3). Then I related this experience:

---

[2] Deuteronomy 1:35-38.
[3] Deuteronomy 1:26-27.
[4] Exodus 14:15-31.
[5] Exodus 16:14-15.
[6] Exodus 13:21-22.

Among these holy sites, the Lord taught me something unique on the banks of the Susquehanna River, in Harmony, Pennsylvania. That general area is where the priesthood was restored to the prophet Joseph Smith by heavenly messengers.[7]

The sacredness of this spot was tangibly felt. For a time, I sat on the banks of that river. I tranquilly watched the subtle waves flowing in peaceful patterns and contemplated all that I had been learning on the tour about the grand gospel of our Great Lord. I thought about the restoration of the Lord's church in our day, the calling of modern-day prophets, and the unparalleled renewal of the Lord's priesthood on the earth. I felt a feeling of awe for the goodness of the Lord and His hand in our lives. In my heart, I found myself asking the same question, "How can people have so many witnesses of the Lord in their lives and yet neglect Him?"

As I sat pondering upon this, the answer came to me as clear as if someone was whispering in my ear. The thought and feeling came over me, "Kayla, it is because they CHOOSE not to Remember."

After relating this experience I had at the Susquehanna River to my patient, he reflectively nodded and then asked me, "Kayla, what does that mean to 'choose not to Remember'?"

I began thumbing through past chapters in the scriptures. As we reviewed them, we highly doubted that the children of Israel (at that time) were becoming extra familiar with the *scriptures*—including the ten commandments the Lord had just revealed to their prophet, Moses. We questioned that the Israelites were *sincerely praying* daily as they should. The idea of them *serving* each other and taking time to be in *sacred places* often was not evident. It was clear that they were not *smiling* or showing *gratitude* for the miracles around them. In essence, it was pretty obvious the children of Israel were not consistently having a 5 Star Day.

---

[7] *Joseph Smith-History* 1:68-72.

As my patient and I went over the other chapters, we were both overcome with the Spirit. That day, my patient began his journey to understand what is meant by the word Remember.

I relayed to my patient, "The Lord symbolically sends 'manna' to each of us day-by-day. He has parted more 'Red Seas' in our lives than we can possibly imagine. God guides us by 'cloud' in the day and 'light' at night. Literally every breath we take is given to us.[8] He is there, leading us to the 'promised land'. Even if it does not feel like it sometimes, God is aware of us. May we choose to *Remember*."

Remember what exactly? Well, when we choose to Remember, we are striving to recollect truths, such as:

- Who we really are, and why we are here on Earth.
- What happens after this life, and the dangers of sin.
- The covenants we have made, and His eternal promises.
- God's hand in our lives, and His miraculous Atonement.
- Past experiences we have had where the Lord taught us His truth, or when we have felt His love through the Holy Ghost, etc.

The simple and vital things in the 5 Star Day help us Remember. We ended our scripture study that day in Deuteronomy Chapter 6. This teaching—as the final verse of our study—pierced our souls:

> And thou shalt love the Lord thy God with all thine heart, and with all thy soul, and with all thy might...Then *beware lest thou forget* the Lord, which brought thee forth out of the land of Egypt, from the house of bondage.[9]

I slowly closed my Bible and looked up at my patient. I repeated his question posed at the beginning, "So, how could the children of Israel act the way they did when it was so evident the Lord was in

---

[8] Mosiah 2:21; Nehemiah 9:6; Helaman 8:24.
[9] Deuteronomy 6:5&12; emphasis added.

their lives?" My patient and I answered in harmony, "Because they were *choosing* every day *not* to Remember."

That scripture study session was a turning point in the life of my patient. From that day forward, he chose to do those essential daily acts that would help him Remember. Even while having a bedridden and machine-dependent body, he rediscovered his faith in God. It was in him all along, he had merely forgotten.

My patient read the Book of Mormon from cover to cover and came to know for himself that it was true. He began praying again. The prophets and apostles speaking in General Conference became one of his favorite semi-annual events. Though he could not attend church, he still chose to keep the Sabbath day holy. He repented of past unholy behaviors, and he chose to share the gospel online often. I had never seen him so happy. He also prepared for his patriarchal blessing, and he received it a few months before I was called to serve a mission in Argentina.

When I received my mission call, my patient and I knew that our time together was limited. It was unknown if he would still be alive when I returned from serving.

I will never forget his face on my last day of work. I was headed home (to another state) to be with my family for a few weeks before entering the Missionary Training Center (the wonderful place where missionaries get trained for six weeks before going to their assigned locations; this place is often called the "MTC"). As we gave each other parting words, my patient said with emotion, "I will be praying for you, Sister Hansen. Thank you for helping me Remember God. Go help the people in Argentina Remember God!" Tears streamed down my face as I waved goodbye.

As a surprise to me, and to everyone who knew him, my patient passed away the week before I entered the MTC. The scriptures teach that when someone dies their spirit goes to a place referred to as the *spirit world*. Their spirit lives on, preparing for the day when their body and spirit are reunited through the resurrection prior to judgement day.[10] (In <u>Chapter 8</u>: Smile Star we talk more about the spirt world; see <u>Chapter 2</u> for resurrection/judgment day). I believe that my patient is now a missionary in the spirit world.[11]

I was humbled and deeply grateful for the miraculous timing that allowed for me to speak at his lovely funeral. The service took place the very day before I entered the MTC. It was clear that my patient began his training as a full-time servant of God at the same time as me. My patient returned home transformed by Christ's Atonement due to his choices to Remember, and to focus on the essential things we ought to be doing daily in order to progress and find Christ's joy and peace in our lives. I am forever grateful for this dear patient and our journey of Remembering.

The Danger in Choosing to Forget

What happens when we choose *not* to Remember? If we are not consciously choosing to Remember daily, it becomes easy for us to forget God's guidance and love over time—i.e. "for our minds to be darkened" or fogged up like the following scripture explains:

> And your minds in times past have been darkened because of unbelief, and because you have treated lightly the things you have received...and this condemnation resteth upon the children of Zion, even all. *And they shall remain under this condemnation until they repent and remember...*[12]

Thankfully, we are only "under this condemnation" (i.e. darkness or lack of progression) until we choose to "repent and remember."[13]

---

[10] Alma 40:12-14; *Doctrine and Covenants* 138; 1 Peter 3:18-20; Luke 16:19-31; Revelation 20:12-13.
[11] 1 Peter 3:18-20; 1 Peter 4:6.
[12] *Doctrine and Covenants* 84:54-59; emphasis added; see Alma 46:8.
[13] *Doctrine and Covenants* 84:57; see Alma 9:8-10.

It can be easy to forget the times the Lord has reached out to us or that we have received witnesses of God's truth. Touching upon this matter, Elder James B. Martino taught:

> I know some who have had undeniable spiritual experiences, but the lack of certain spiritual habits seems to have caused them to forget the times when God has spoken to them.
>
> To those...and to all of us, if you 'have felt to sing the song of redeeming love, I would ask, can ye feel so now?' If you do not feel it now, you can feel it again.…Be obedient, remember the times when you have felt the Spirit in the past, and ask in faith. Your answer will come, and you will feel the love and peace of the Savior. It may not come as quickly or in the format you desire, but the answer will come. Do not give up! Never give up![14]

Prophets of all ages (and the Lord Himself) have repeatedly cried out, "*O, remember, remember!*" [15]

I have learned that testimony and conversion are a process over a lifetime of choosing to Remember. Marian, a dear elderly friend of mine, has been an amazing example to me throughout my life. The first Sunday of the month is called Fast Sunday. During that day, anyone who desires to bear their testimony of Christ and His gospel is invited to come up to the pulpit to share their testimony with the congregation. When I was a little girl, Marian chose to walk up to the pulpit on Fast Sunday and humbly bear her testimony of Christ nearly every month. Advanced age had caused for a lot of health challenges and the need for a cane. Sometimes she could not make the walk to the pulpit, so a microphone was brought to her as she stood in her pew. Regardless, she would valiantly bear testimony of

---

[14] James B. Martino, "Turn to Him and Answers Will Come," *Ensign*, Nov. 2015, 58-60.
[15] Alma 37:13&35; *Doctrine and Covenants* 3:3; Helaman 5:6-9&12; Mosiah 2:41; Isaiah 49:14-16; 2 Nephi 30:6; emphasis added.

truth. When she stood and declared the truths she held so dear, the room was filled with the Holy Spirit every time.

Marian once made mention to the idea that she was born with a testimony. She expressed something along the lines that when we have moments in which we feel the Spirit confirming truth, perhaps these are moments that we are not so much *gaining a testimony* as they are moments in which we *recognize and Remember that we already have one.*

My sisters and I have studied and pondered upon this, and we believe her comment is very insightful. Before we came to the earth, we already knew Christ and Heavenly Father, and we already accepted their plan. When we bear our testimonies and cultivate them continually, we are able to Remember and to keep growing.

It is important to recognize that there is a divine difference between testimony and conversion. *Testimony* is a foundation of belief that comes as we receive witnesses from the Holy Ghost of truth.[16] What we do with that testimony is the process of *conversion* (the process of becoming a true disciple of Jesus Christ).[17] Clearly, in many ways we can still use the phrase "gain a testimony" to refer to our spiritual progression, but Remembrance is the key and conversion is the process.

Heritage Tours: CTR

The experience I shared with my patient, that took place along the banks of the Susquehanna River, was a part of the incredible church history tour called Heritage Tours.[18] I think the name in itself is significant. How great a need we each have to be connected to and Remember our heritage, especially our Heavenly heritage!

---

[16] Dieter F. Uchtdorf, "The Power of a Personal Testimony," *Ensign*, 37-39.
[17] David A. Bednar, "Converted Unto the Lord," *Ensign*, Nov. 2012, 106-109.
[18] Heritage Tours—An Experience in Travel, *ldsheritagetours.com* (accessed July 1, 2017).

This expedition allowed for what was called "an experience in travel." Again, we visited historical sites where significant spiritual events had taken place in the life of Joseph Smith and the early saints of Christ's restored gospel. The profound experiences I had while on that church history tour have continued to have an effect on my day-to-day life.

I bear solemn testimony that I know that Joseph Smith was called as the Lord's prophet to restore Christ's gospel in full. I have walked the paths that Joseph walked, and the Spirit testified to me of the truthfulness of what God called him to do. I cannot deny how I *felt*.

Paraphrasing these song lyrics best describes the experience: "I *felt* hope, I *felt* love, I *felt* peace within my soul, I *felt* strength from above, and *I knew I was not alone*."[19]

While coming to experience these truths for myself on the tour, our incredible tour guides repeatedly taught us about the significant acronym **CTR** (**C**hoose **T**he **R**ight). Wearing a ring on one's finger with the inscription "CTR" is a common thing among members of the church as a reminder to make good choices and follow the Savior. Our tour guides took this acronym and they powerfully expounded upon it. With each new site, they introduced significant additional meanings of the acronym CTR. I am not going to share them all, but I have felt to share three important examples; please pay attention to the way you feel as you read them. I know that the gift of remembrance can be felt when we read these examples with a sincere heart.

---

[19] Jeff Sermon, "The Way We Feel," song #5, *ldsheritagetours.com* (accessed Nov. 19, 2016); see Galatians 5:22-23.

Example 1: Continue The Rescue (CTR)

With the restoration of Christ's gospel upon the earth came also the eventual call for the saints to move westward, away from the persecution and mobs in the New England areas (Satan is the worst). The early saints of Christ's restored church—aka the *pioneers*—traveled over 1,300 miles to a land they did not know (now known as Salt Lake Valley, Utah), and they walked by faith through their trusting in God's guidance given to His prophet. The pioneers suffered extreme afflictions, and their love and dedication to God was awe-inspiring.

During a particular group's trek west (the Martin Handcart Company), they underwent severe winter challenges. Many froze to death and others died of starvation. Sometimes the ground was too frozen to even bury their dead. In these winter conditions these pioneers traveled by foot while pulling handcarts, crossing many terribly cold rivers along the way. When this group arrived to the icy Sweetwater River in Wyoming, they could not gather the strength to cross it. After all they had been through, the mere sight of this river caused grown men to fall to their knees and cry.[20]

To this company's great astonishment, a small group of rescuers showed up (some in their late teenage years). Those who had already made it to the Salt Lake Valley heard of the dire situation of those who were crossing the plains that winter, and many chose to answer the call to rescue and help. These valiant men helped carry, one-by-one, the members of this disheartened company of pioneers across the river. It has been noted that, in later years, many of these young rescuers died from the effects of this heroic effort.[21]

As I stood on the ground near the Sweetwater River, we were taught the choice that we now have to **C**ontinue **T**he **R**escue (CTR).

---

[20] Gordon B. Hinckley, "Four B's for Boys," *Ensign*, Oct. 1981, *lds.org* (accessed July 7, 2016).
[21] Chad M. Orton, "The Martin Handcart Company at the Sweetwater: Another Look," *byustudies.byu.edu* (accessed July 17, 2016).

Our tour guides reminded us that God asks that we lift one another, help each other home, share His gospel, and love His children.[22] Will we answer the call and continue the rescue? O Remember![23]

Sooner or later we will each need a lift across the "Sweetwater Rivers" in our own lives as well. God will not leave us. The Lord will send help. We matter to Him, and He will **Continue The Rescue!**[24] God does not allow for us to pass through hardships so that He can *punish us;* rather, so that He can *refine us, if we let Him.*[25]

I will never forget the way that I felt as I looked out on the Sweetwater River in remembrance of the pioneers' legacy of faith and love. It was as if the wind itself was carrying the subtle message from the saints of the past, "Kayla, please remember us! Oh Kayla, please **Continue The Rescue!**" That call still rings within my soul.

Oh, please *Remember.*

Example 2: Cross The River (CTR)

This second CTR requires a step back into history (before the pioneers headed west). Like I said before, the saints were repeatedly harassed by mobs and were driven out of their homes and cities. With time, they ended up settling in Nauvoo, Illinois, for several years until the Lord called for their trek west.

While in Nauvoo, they worked hard and were led by the prophet Joseph Smith in making that swampy land into a beautiful and productive city. God commanded the saints to build a temple there (we will talk more about the significance of temples later in this chapter). After several years of considerable peace and wonderful labor, the enemies of Christ's restored gospel began persecuting the saints again to a relentless point. Joseph was by no means perfect,

---

22 *Doctrine and Covenants* 81:5; Mosiah 18:8-10; John 14:16-18; John 13:34-35.

23 Alma 29:10-13.

24 Ronald A. Rasband, "The Joyful Burden of Discipleship," *Ensign*, May 2014, 9-11; also see John 14:16-18; John 13:34-35, Jacob 5:41&47.

25 James E. Faust, "The Refiner's Fire," *Ensign*, May 1979, *lds.org* (accessed May 9, 2016).

but he was innocent of the charges against him.[26] He heroically delivered himself into the hands of these persecutors with the hope to be able to appease the oppression of the saints. The dear, beloved prophet, Joseph Smith, was taken and held as prisoner at Carthage Jail (in Carthage, Illinois), along with three other innocent, faithful men (one of them being Joseph's brother, Hyrum).

Joseph knew his mortal life would soon come to a close. He wrote, "I am going like a lamb to the slaughter; but I am calm as a summer's morning; I have a conscience void of offense toward God, and toward all men."[27] Joseph's premonition was right. The jail was ambushed, and he and Hyrum were killed by men poisoned with false rumors (lies of Satan). As protectors of the saints and defenders of truth and righteousness, Joseph and Hyrum sealed their testimonies of Jesus Christ with their very lives.[28]

I know with all my heart that Joseph Smith was called to restore Christ's church here on the earth. I feel the Holy Ghost testify of this glorious truth every time I read about his experience in the Sacred Grove (refer to chapter 3).[29] It really happened. Christ continued his pattern of calling prophets and apostles to lead and guide us. I cannot deny it. Due to his kindness, joyful personality, and charity toward all, the saints endearingly called the prophet "Brother Joseph." As I have come to learn of his divine calling and genuine characteristics, Joseph Smith has become "Brother Joseph" to me as well.

I have been to Carthage Jail, and I have stood at the very window where they shot Joseph. As I gazed out this window, my gratitude for the prophet Joseph Smith overcame me. After waiting for the other people to leave the room, I leaned my head against the left side of the window frame and then I wept inconsolably in a way

---

[26] Dallin H. Oaks, "Joseph, the Man and the Prophet," *Ensign*, April 1996, *lds.org* (accessed June 3, 2016).
[27] *Doctrine and Covenants* 135:1-7.
[28] Jeffrey R. Holland, "Safety For the Soul," *Ensign*, Nov. 2009, 88-90.
[29] *Joseph Smith-History* 1:10-17.

that I have never cried before. It was not until later that I realized that there was one other girl in the room. She was weeping on the right side of the window frame. Oh, please *Remember.*

The mob thought that they could stop the Lord's work by killing Joseph Smith. They were deceived. The ordained apostles carried on the priesthood authority to guide Jesus Christ's church.[30] The senior apostle, Brigham Young, was the next sustained prophet.[31] Nobody could, can, or will stop this work, because it is not of man, it is of God.[32]

Shortly following the martyrdom of Joseph Smith, a very large number of the saints answered the sacred call to make the trek west in order to establish Zion (i.e. the pure in heart or the Lord's people) away from the persecutions.[33] Most had faith and hope in the continued priesthood authority through the twelve apostles and the Lord's newly sustained prophet, but they truly mourned the loss of their dear Brother Joseph.

With heavy hearts and few resources, the saints exited Nauvoo by way of a dirt road called Parley Street. As they walked down this gravely road, I imagine the winter wind chilled them and many tears were shed.[34] They were leaving their blessed city, beloved temple, and their homes. They had worked hard, grown, and thrived there beyond measure. But now they were asked to say goodbye. As they left their beloved city, the glorious Nauvoo Temple could be seen from the path as they made their way to the Mississippi River (the winter climate had completely frozen the river over). *Parley Street ends at the Mississippi River; at this point, the saints had a choice to make.* They could turn back to Nauvoo, or they could follow the call of the Lord and choose to **C**ross **T**he **R**iver (CTR).

---

[30] *Doctrine and Covenants* 107:23&33-35; *Doctrine and Covenants* 112:21&30-32.

[31] *Doctrine and Covenants* 124:127-128; "Brigham Young Leads the Church": *Doctrine and Covenants and Church History*, (1997), 216-221.

[32] Daniel 2:35; *History of the Church*, 4:540; 2 Nephi 30:3-8.

[33] *Doctrine and Covenants* 97:21; *Doctrine and Covenants* 82:14; Isaiah 2:2-3.

[34] "The Trail of Hope: Exodus from Nauvoo," *Ensign*, July 2013, 40-43.

I have walked the gravely road on Parley Street. Every few yards there are signs with quotes from pioneers that left that dear city—including a quote from my own ancestor. With each new quote, my eyes wet with tears. I could feel of their sorrow and could imagine their devastation. Their courage, faith, and devotion to the Lord was incredible. As I made my way to the end of Parley Street, I stood on the banks of the great Mississippi River. The wind rustled through my hair as I gazed across this grand river. I felt the question swell up within my heart, "Would you have crossed the river?"

I imagined the pioneers, and my ancestors, standing at the banks of this very river. As the cold winter wind rustled through their hair, they must have carried a weight of uncertainty for the future. Have you ever felt that way? Nonetheless, they realized that everything they had (even their families) was given to them from God. They had a sure hope that the Lord had a plan and a land prepared for them, and so they pressed forward. These courageous saints made their way to the end of Parley Street, and they valiantly chose to **C**ross **T**he **R**iver. Is some of their courage and faith left in us? [35] Yes, it is.

Since that day, I have symbolically stood before the frozen "Mississippi River" many times in my life. I have had situations and calls from the Lord that have not always been easy, convenient, or what I planned for in my life. It is a part of our experience and growth here on Earth that we are called to do and endure things that are hard. With each experience, we have the same choice as the pioneers. Will we **C**ross **T**he **R**iver? Will we choose to follow the prophets and follow the pathway of Christ no matter the sacrifices, uncertainty, or cost? May we be able to answer the Lord's call to **C**ross **T**he **R**iver during the course of each of our lives.

Oh, please *Remember.*

---

[35] "Heritage—We'll Be There," *song 3*, Sam Payne; *ldsheritagetours.com* (accessed July 5, 2016).

Example 3: Choose To Remember (CTR)

The last thing I feel to share from this wonderful tour was the overarching theme of the trip.

As we ended our journey, we were each given a coin with the words: Remember, Remember, Remember. Our main tour guide, Bob Eliason, taught us that the first Remember was the smallest because it was the least important, and it was to prompt us to *Remember what we saw.* The second Remember was more important than the first, and was to prompt us to *Remember what we learned.* The final Remember was the most important. It was there to prompt us to *Remember how we felt.* **C**hoose **T**o **R**emember (CTR).

I realized that Brother Eliason was right. I have knelt in prayer in the Sacred Grove where Heavenly Father and Jesus Christ appeared to the prophet Joseph Smith. I have a small recollection of what that grove looks like and I can recall a few things I learned there, but above all, I can Remember without a shadow of a doubt how I felt there. I felt the confirming feelings of joy, peace, and hope from the Holy Ghost.[36] I have no doubt that what Joseph said happened there truly did. His humble prayer in that grove of trees changed the world. **C**hoose **T**o **R**emember.

As I began to think back on each individual site, I realized that the same pattern was observed with all of them. If I tried really hard to remember what the areas looked like, I could recollect very little. If I really pushed my mind to recall what I learned, I could think of a few things. In contrast, when I exerted all I could to Remember how I felt, I could feel the Spirit engulf me as if I was at that site again.

With this realization, I learned that I did not need to be on this tour in order to come to know that these things are true. The Holy Ghost teaches us in such a way that we can feel God's truth as we

---

[36] Galatians 5:22-23.

study, act, and **C**hoose **T**o **R**emember. We can Remember and come to know for ourselves that these things are true regardless if we have been to these literal locations or not.

You do not have to stand on the banks of the Red Sea to feel the Spirit testify that Moses parted it by the power of God.[37] You do not have to kneel in the Sacred Grove in order to come to know for yourself if Joseph Smith truly was called as a prophet.[38] You do not need to stand on the holy soil in the Garden of Gethsemane in order to feel and know that Christ atoned for you or stand at the Garden Tomb to know that He was resurrected.[39] The Spirit can bring to our life this gift of Remembrance if we make the effort to **C**hoose **T**o **R**emember.

The best part is that as we strive to Remember, the Lord helps us Remember. As we put forth diligent and honest effort, God will "[enlarge] our memory," our "mind doth begin to expand," and the Holy Ghost brings "all things unto remembrance."[40] We can do it!

The experiences I had on that tour are given little value by me if I do not apply what I learned—if I do not **C**hoose **T**o **R**emember. I hope that these past three examples stirred some Remembrance of the Lord's love for you and Remembrance of valiant souls who have gone before you. They cry unto us to please *Remember* and *be faithful!*

*Continue **T**he **R**escue. **C**ross **T**he **R**iver. **C**hoose **T**o **R**emember.*

Taking time to Remember our heritage is a part of the Sacred Time Star. More than anything, taking time to Remember God's hand in our daily lives, and the witnesses we have already received of His truths, brings added power into our earthly experience.[41] In

[37] Exodus 14:15-31.
[38] *Joseph Smith-History* 1:16-19.
[39] Luke 22:39-46; John 20:3-18.
[40] Alma 37:8; Alma 32:34; John 14:26.
[41] Helaman 8:24.

order to more fully feel this power, we must take time to "be still" and "reconnect with heaven."[42]

Certain places can facilitate the experience of the Sacred Time Star, and some activities can assist us. Our Sacred Time Star will not be the same every day.

Two irreplaceable sacred places we need to prioritize are: church and the temple. If we allow it, these holy spots can be powerful at facilitating our need to reconnect and Remember. This is a huge part of the reason why the Lord created these two holy places.

The Kingdom of God on the Earth

I recall many times growing up that I was not the biggest fan of sacrament meeting (the first hour of church in which we listen to speakers and partake of the sacrament). I survived on cheerios and coloring pages in order to endure what seemed like "years" of endless talks each week. There are days that we may feel that way in our adulthood too. In the prime of my adult years, I have totally "borrowed" crackers from little kiddos. Please don't tell.

However, the condition of my heart, in terms of church service, has changed drastically over the years. Sunday has become my most cherished day of the week. I even enjoy sacrament meeting, a lot actually. Church has become one of my favorite Sacred Time Stars of the week, and it is truly irreplaceable.

Church worship provides us with opportunities to review truths, renew covenants, teach, learn, grow, serve, reconnect with heaven, and Remember. In modern-day revelation the Lord commanded:

> And that thou mayest more fully keep thyself unspotted
> from the world, thou shalt go to the house of prayer and
> offer up thy sacraments upon my holy day; for verily this is

---

[42] Psalms 46:10; "Be Still, My Soul," *Hymns*, no. 124.

a day appointed unto you to rest from your labors, and to pay thy devotions unto the Most High.[43]

Sundays are a day to reconnect, refocus, and Remember. God taught us that keeping the Sabbath day holy is a commandment.[44] Partaking in church service is not just a kind suggestion; rather, it is a key part of the holiness of that day so we can be renewed weekly.

Those who work on an occasional Sunday—including those in the medical field—can do everything in their power to make Sunday a different day from the rest. Also, they can strive to make the effort to plan their break during a nearby church's sacrament meeting. That way they can still partake of the sacrament.

The sacrament is a renewal of our baptismal covenants—or promises we made with God at baptism. When we are baptized we are showing that we are willing to diligently strive to be like Christ, always remember Him, keep His commandments, and serve Him to the end.[45] If we keep these covenants, God promises that we will be completely cleansed from sin, "spiritually [reborn]," and we will receive the gift of the Holy Ghost.[46]

Baptism is not complete without the reception of the gift of the Holy Ghost.[47] President Wilford Woodruff taught that this gift "is the greatest gift that can be bestowed upon man."[48] Before baptism, we can *occasionally* feel the comfort and guidance of the Holy Ghost as we attend church, read the scriptures, pray, serve, etc. After baptism, we can have the companionship of the Holy Ghost with us *always*. You receive it by priesthood holders laying their hands on your head and confirming this gift upon you. In that confirmation, you hear the powerful exhortation: "Receive the Holy Ghost." Once you and I have received this gift, we cannot obtain it passively; we

---

[43] *Doctrine and Covenants* 59:9-10.
[44] Exodus 20:8-11.
[45] Mosiah 18:8-10; *Doctrine and Covenants* 20:37; Romans 6:3-6; 2 Nephi 31:4-13&17.
[46] John 3:3-7; Romans 6:3-6; Mosiah 5:2; 2 Nephi 31:4-13; Acts 2:37-38; Matthew 3:13-17.
[47] Acts 2:37-38; *Doctrine and Covenants* 33:15; 2 Nephi 32:5; Acts 19:1-7; 3 Nephi 19:9-13.
[48] *Deseret Weekly*, April 6, 1889, 451.

"receive the Holy Ghost" in our lives day-to-day through the good choices we make.[49] The 5 Star Day helps us receive the Holy Ghost.

The sacrament involves both bread and water. The broken bread represents Christ's body—in every aspect of His life, death, and resurrection.[50] The water represents the blood that He shed to atone for our sins.[51] An "if and then" clause is noted in the sacramental promise. We recommit to "always remember Him," "take His name upon us" (strive to be like Jesus), and "keep His commandments."[52] If we do these things, then we are qualified for this promise: "[We] may always have His Spirit to be with [us]."[53]

Elder Dallin H. Oaks taught, "[The] Spirit is the foundation of our testimony. It testifies of the Father and the Son, brings all things to our remembrance, and leads us into truth. It is the compass to guide us on our path."[54] How we need this gift daily!

With nothing but love in my heart, I extend an invitation. If you have not been baptized (and received the gift of the Holy Ghost) by someone holding the restored priesthood, I invite you to prepare to do so. These are some of the most glorious and important actions you will ever partake in. Remember, these are two of the essential steps necessary in your journey home, and they will guide you in becoming who you are meant to become (see Chapter 2).

If you have already done these things, do you Remember how pure and clean you felt that day? Wouldn't it be nice to be baptized every week? Well, that is essentially what is happening when we partake of the sacrament! We can have a clean slate every week.[55]

After we are baptized, we still make many daily mistakes. We desperately need the sacrament in order to fully access the Savior's

---

[49] David A. Bednar, "Receive the Holy Ghost," *Ensign*, Nov. 2010, 94-97; see Acts 2:37-38.
[50] 1 Corinthians 11:23-25.
[51] Luke 22:19-20.
[52] *Doctrine and Covenants* 20:77; Moroni 4-5.
[53] John 6:54; Moroni 4:3; Moroni 5:2; 3 Nephi 18:1-11.
[54] Dallin H. Oaks, "Sacrament Meeting and the Sacrament," *Ensign*, Nov. 2008, 17-18.
[55] David A. Bednar, "Always Retain a Remission of Your Sins," *Ensign*, May 2016, 59-62.

Atonement, and to be found clean to enter God's presence.[56] A modern-day apostle, Dallin H. Oaks, taught:

> The ordinance of the sacrament makes the sacrament meeting the most sacred and important meeting in the Church. I sense that some…have not yet come to understand the significance of this meeting and the importance of individual reverence and worship in it.[57]

God is a God of order. By studying His patterns, we can see that the Lord is also a fan of teamwork. Due to this, think of how many meetings take place in the Lord's church.

To name just a few, there are: relief society, primary, priesthood, stake, bishopric, high council, Seventies, First Presidency, and Twelve Apostle meetings, etc. And yet, Elder Oaks confirms that of all the holy meetings in the Lord's church, sacrament meeting is the most important. *But why?* After all that we have been discussing, focus on what is one of the fundamental words in renewing our covenants (or promises) during the sacrament.

While breaking the bread for the sacrament, the Savior Himself taught, "And this shall ye do in *remembrance* of my body, which I have shown unto you. And it shall be a testimony unto the Father that ye do always *remember* me. And if ye do always *remember* me ye shall have my Spirit to be with you."[58]

As the second part of the sacrament was administered, Christ taught, "And this shall ye always do to those who repent and are baptized in my name; and ye shall do it in *remembrance* of my blood, which I have shed for you, that ye may witness unto the Father that ye do always *remember* me. And if ye do always *remember* me ye shall have my Spirit to be with you."[59] The Savior pleads for us to take time every week to *Remember* that He gave Himself a ransom for our

[56] John 6:54; 3 Nephi 18:1-11; Matthew 26:26-28.
[57] Dallin H. Oaks, "Sacrament Meeting and the Sacrament," *Ensign*, Nov. 2008, 17-18.
[58] 3 Nephi 18:7; emphasis added; Luke 22:19; *Doctrine and Covenants* 20:75-79.
[59] 3 Nephi 18:11; emphasis added; Luke 22:20; see also *Doctrine and Covenants* 20:75-79.

sins.[60] When I see the white tablecloth that covers the bread and water, it reminds me of the cloth covering Christ's body in the tomb. He died for and paid the debt personally for you. Oh, please *Remember.*

While the sacrament is being passed it can be a Sacred Time moment, a time to connect with heaven. We can close our eyes and say a prayer—renewing all our covenants and asking for forgiveness. We can review the lyrics of the sacrament hymn, read a scripture about His Atonement, or picture Christ in our minds. It is a Sacred Time moment to refocus, to reflect, and to Remember Him.

May we recollect why this is such a big deal. I hope that none of us partake of the sacrament lightly. If at this time we are not yet worthy to partake of the sacrament, let's get back on track! You are capable and worth it! He died for you.

My sister, Janessa, has told me often, "Kayla, I can never repay the Savior for what He has done for me, but I can strive to always Remember Him." Wow. I love that.

My sister, Ashton, noted, "Our thoughts influence our emotions, our emotions influence our actions, and our actions determine our destiny. If Christ is the focus of every thought, how different will our emotions, actions, and destiny be? This puts the sacrament and all other covenants in perspective for me. It makes sense why the Lord asks us to 'look unto [Him] in every thought' and to always Remember Him."[61] What an insightful connection.

Going to church to partake of the sacrament (1st hour) and participate in other edifying classes (2nd hour: Sunday School, and 3rd hour: men and women split up into Relief Society and Priesthood classes) truly can refill our "spiritual bucket." These three hours can vary in which order they are in, but all three hours are so important and beneficial! Make them all a priority! There are classes specifically

[60] 1 Timothy 2:5-6; Alma 42:16-18&22-26; *Doctrine and Covenants* 19:16-19; Luke 22:41-44.
[61] *Doctrine and Covenants* 6:36; Moroni 5:2; Luke 22:19.

for toddlers, children, and teenagers as well.[62] What a blessing to be able to help and serve each other in this journey of learning Christ's truths for ourselves. We can gain so much from each hour because they can offer distinct opportunities for our spiritual growth.

How can we allow for church service to fulfill our Sacred Time Star need of the day? These three aids assist us in having a heavenly reconnection at church: *preparation*, *dress*, and a *willingness to learn*.

Preparation

We can prepare ourselves to reconnect with heaven. President Nelson taught, "[We each bear] responsibility for the spiritual enrichment that can come from a sacrament meeting." He urges the benefit of getting there early, and prayerfully listening to the prelude music: "During that interval, prelude music is subdued. This is not a time for conversation or transmission of messages but a period of prayerful meditation as leaders and members prepare spiritually for the sacrament."[63] President Boyd K. Packer taught that "prelude music, reverently played, is nourishment for the spirit…it invites inspiration."[64]

The local congregations that meet together for church are called *wards* or *ward families*. During my years studying at BYU-Idaho, I was able to attend church at several student wards. With each new ward I would grow in different ways. They were all wonderful, but there was one ward in particular that I will never forget.

In that ward, the bishop took the pre-sacrament preparation admonition from President Nelson seriously, and he implemented it strongly. The first week of the semester, I arrived to the sacrament room and there was the typical orchestra of light-minded chitchat that tends to go on before sacrament meeting starts. Another usual happening was that a good portion of the ward came trickling in

---

[62] *lds.org/callings/primary*; *lds.org/youth* (accessed July 7, 2017).
[63] Russell M. Nelson, "Worshiping at Sacrament Meeting," *Ensign*, Aug. 2004, 27.
[64] Boyd K. Packer, "Personal Revelation: The Gift, the Test, and the Promise," *Ensign*, Nov. 1994, 61.

late. Due to the regularity of these things, I did not think anything of it as we started sacrament meeting.

At the end of the hour, the bishop got up to speak. He humbly and powerfully bore testimony of the deeper magnitude the Spirit would have in our lives, and in our ward, if we followed the inspired direction to arrive early and quietly prepare our hearts and minds to participate in the sacrament.

Our Bishop and his counselors repeatedly reminded us of this goal throughout the weeks and months. Not only did they remind us but they lived it themselves. They came early and would quietly read their scriptures, preparing their minds for the sacred ordinance. Our ward began to change. In time, the majority of the ward began to come fifteen minutes early. It was a rarity for anyone to show up late. After this transformation, I recall walking into this ward's sacrament room and feeling an overabundant sense of peace every week.

We were not anti-social zombies. We greeted each other silently and with smiles during our preparations. After sacrament meeting, our ward members and bishopric were very friendly and welcoming to all. A greater abundance of the Spirit filled all three meetings, and there was a deeper spiritual maturity and unity felt.

Also, I experienced an enhanced guidance in my school studies and day-to-day life that semester. That bishop's promise truly was from God, and it was fulfilled through our faithfulness.

It is also of great worth to study the Sunday lessons beforehand for greater preparedness. We will have times in our lives that are easier than others to get to church on time, prayerfully listen to the prelude music, and prepare for the lessons prior to church starting. However, it is as President Russell M. Nelson has said, "Don't demand things that are unreasonable, but demand of yourself improvement."[65]

---

[65] Russell M. Nelson, "Men's Hearts Shall Fail Them," *Mormon Messages*.

Sometimes I get out of the habit of coming to church early and spiritually preparing beforehand. Thankfully new beginnings are real. When I choose to reestablish these preparation patterns into my Sunday worship, my spiritual experiences are magnified and my "spiritual bucket" is more fully filled every Sunday.

Dress

I have had the opportunity to go to church in places all over the United States and also in Argentina. The condition of our hearts in our choice of attire going to church is more important than the clothing itself.

There are benefits to and reasons behind why we are encouraged to dress respectfully in holy places. Elder Oaks relayed, "Our manner of dress indicates the degree to which we understand and honor the ordinance in which we will participate."[66] Elder Holland said priesthood holders should live worthy to partake of and administer the sacrament. He insightfully included this neat parallel:

> May I suggest that wherever possible a white shirt be worn by the deacons, teachers, and priests who handle the sacrament. For sacred ordinances in the Church we often use ceremonial clothing, and a white shirt could be seen as gentle reminder of the white clothing you wore in the baptismal font and an anticipation of the white shirt you will soon wear into the temple and onto your missions.[67]

When we remember what sacred ordinance we are partaking in, it becomes natural to want to wear clothes that show reverence and respect. Typically when we think of our "Sunday best" attire we think of dresses, skirts, and blouses. Also white shirts and ties with suit coats. I have learned that if the best we sincerely have to wear to

---

[66] Dallin H. Oaks, "Sacrament Meeting and the Sacrament," *Ensign*, Nov. 2008, 17-19.
[67] Jeffrey R. Holland, "This Do in Remembrance of Me," *Ensign*, Nov. 1995, 68.

church are sweat pants and a stained white T-shirt, the Lord appreciates our efforts. He appreciates us being there!

Whether at church or not, the Lord desires for women and men to dress respectfully and modestly.[68] Our Father asks this of us because He loves us—for truly our bodies are temples.[69] Dressing modestly helps ourselves and others to look at us for who we are as sons and daughters of God.

With some of those thoughts in mind, what you choose to wear is between you and the Lord. He wants you there, that is more important than what you wear.

Willingness to Learn

How many times have you received an answer to one of your prayers while you were at church? The Lord can answer us through the talks given in sacrament meeting and in the other classes. *The Spirit* can answer our soul's prayer. We can receive this direction through willingness to listen and learn. We can often times obtain the answers we seek, even if the talks technically have little to do with the questions we have. *Receiving answers* to prayer can happen often while at church. More than anything, *gaining peace* from church worship can and should happen weekly.

We are taught that "the Lord requireth the heart and a willing mind."[70] We are learning and growing together in the Lord's gospel. Willingness includes eliminating distractions. I know that if we apply what Elder Dallin H. Oaks counsels us in the following quote our spiritual lives will be enriched significantly. He exhorted:

> During [church]—and especially during the sacrament
> service—we should concentrate on worship and refrain
> from all other activities, especially from behavior that could

---

[68] "Dress and Appearance," *For the Strength of Youth*, 6-8.
[69] 1 Corinthians 6:19-20.
[70] *Doctrine and Covenants* 64:34.

interfere with the worship of others…Young people, it is not a time for whispered conversations on cell phones or for texting persons at other locations. When we partake of the sacrament, we make a sacred covenant that we will always remember the Savior. How sad to see persons obviously violating that covenant in the very meeting where they are making it.[71]

Now, you could potentially say, "Kayla, trying to keep my kids to sit still during church is pretty distracting for me." Helping establish your children's lives upon gospel habits is a worthwhile distraction.[72] Hang in there! Keep coming! Consistency brings miracles.

At times we may come to church ready to learn, with distractions eliminated to the best of our abilities, and we are in need of some spiritual nourishment. As the talks and lessons begin, we may soon come to find that the topics being taught are not quite what we thought we needed. What then? Someone once asked the prophet Spencer W. Kimball, "What do you do when you find yourself in a boring sacrament meeting?" His answer was powerful, "I don't know. I've never been in one."[73] This demonstrates that as we allow the Holy Spirit to be our teacher, we can refill our "spiritual buckets" each Sunday regardless of the speakers and the topics. A significant reminder was once shared with me:

> Remember the purpose of studying the gospel is to convert us, to change us, to make us more like the Savior. That only happens if we make connections between the gospel and our personal lives. [During] class, share your experiences, and ask questions. Ponder why the gospel matters to you.[74]

---

[71] Dallin H. Oaks, "Sacrament Meeting and the Sacrament," *Ensign*, Nov. 2008, 17-20.
[72] Proverbs 22:6; Alma 37:6; *Doctrine and Covenants* 68:25-28; Alma 56:47; Alma 57:21.
[73] Donald L. Hallstrom, "Converted to His Gospel through His Church," *Ensign*, May 2012, 15.
[74] Ted Barnes, "How to Never Have a Boring Church Class Again," *New Era*, Jan. 2013, *lds.org*, The Church of Jesus Christ of Latter-day Saints, Jan. 2013 (accessed June 5, 2016).

I know from personal experience that when we implement preparedness, dress, and a willingness to learn into our weekly church experiences, we will be able to Remember the Lord's goodness, truly renew our covenants, and we will refill our "spiritual buckets" every Sunday. That is truly a worthwhile and essential Sacred Time Star of the week. May we not take the vitality and gift of Sunday worship lightly. *Reconnect and Remember.*

The House of the Lord

I want to briefly talk about the other primary place that we ought to have our Sacred Time moment of the day as often as possible. This holy place is the temple of God.

Ever since the Old Testament, New Testament, and subsequent Book of Mormon times, the Lord has *always* commanded His people to build temples and to make higher covenants with Him.[75] Again, covenants are promises made between us and the Lord. Covenants protect us. God gives us certain blessings as we promise to keep our end of the deal.[76] For example, we just talked about how we make covenants when we are baptized; we renew them weekly during the sacrament. Temples are sacred structures where God can guide, teach, and bless His children, and above all where we can make more covenants after baptism. These higher covenants made only in temples make it possible to have *eternal families.*[77]

Sadly, due to the Great Apostasy (see Chapter 3), there were no temples found on the earth for many centuries.[78] When Christ's gospel was restored, the Lord naturally commanded His people to

---

[75] Exodus 26-27; 2 Chronicles 5:1-14; Ezra 3:1-13; Luke 2:40-49; Matthew 21:10-14; 2 Nephi 5:16; Mosiah 1:18.

[76] Judges 2:1; *Doctrine and Covenants* 82:10; Jeremiah 31:31-34; Galatians 3: 26-29.

[77] Exodus 26-27; 2 Chronicles 5:1-14; Ezra 3:1-13; Luke 2:40-49; Matthew 21:10-14; 2 Nephi 5:16; Mosiah 1:18; 3 Nephi 11:1.

[78] Matthew 27:51; Luke 21:6; Mark 13:1-2.

again build temples! In this marvelous age in which we live, we have more than 155 temples throughout the world, and the number is growing year by year![79] How amazing is that? What a blessing. More and more people are being given the opportunity to live where regular temple worship is a possibility.

To recap, because of the restoration of Christ's gospel we can have a place of peace and learning, and above all, a place where we can receive the covenants necessary to have *eternal families*. Without temples there could be no eternal families.

I want to live with my family and friends forever. "No Empty Chairs" is one of my family's mottos. We want "No Empty Chairs" in the temple and in the kingdom of God.[80] We are all meant to be there. We can do it! The prophet, Thomas S. Monson, declared after the death of his sweet wife, Frances:

> Of utmost comfort to me during this tender time of parting have been my testimony of the gospel of Jesus Christ and the knowledge I have that my dear Frances lives still. I know that our separation is temporary. We were sealed in the house of God by one having authority to bind on earth and in heaven. I know that we will be reunited one day and will never again be separated. This is the knowledge that sustains me.[81]

President Monson is able to bear this solemn testimony because he has been sealed to his wife and family in the holy temple. If they hold true to their end of the covenant, they will be *eternally* linked together. Death is a necessary "doorway" until they shall be reunited in the next life. If they have each lived faithful to the pathway of

---

[79] "Why Latter-day Saints build Temples," *lds.org* (accessed Jan 7. 2016); *Doctrine and Covenants* 95; *Doctrine and Covenants* 109; *Doctrine and Covenants* 124.
[80] "No Empty Chairs," Music and lyrics by Janice Kapp Perry & Senator Orrin Hatch, *Jesus' Love Is Like a River*, 1998.
[81] Thomas S. Monson, "I Will Not Fail Thee, nor Forsake Thee," *Ensign*, Nov. 2013, 85-87.

Jesus Christ, they shall inherit the kingdom of God together. No Empty Chairs.

The things that take place in the temple are sacred. We do not have to be "perfect" to enter the temple; Christ was the only perfect Being to ever live and it is through Him that we may become worthy to enter His house. In order to enter the temple, we must be striving to keep the Lord's commandments and to observe and keep our baptismal covenants. After we certify our worthiness in interviews with our local priesthood leaders, we may receive a *temple recommend* that allows us to enter the temple.[82] Whenever a new temple is built there is a period of time where *all people* can come and see what is inside of the temple and learn more about it. I invite you to attend any newly built temple's Open House.[83] After a few months, the temple will be dedicated unto the Lord by one of His prophets or apostles, and from that day forward only those holding a temple recommend can enter. God is a God of order, and temple work can be pure joy.

Many of us have temples nearby. Some have a temple within an hour of their homes, and there are others who have a temple within a few minutes of their homes! It is amazing!

With your given circumstances, prayerfully make a commitment with the Lord to go to the temple for your Sacred Time moment of the day often. With the personal revelation received, you will be able to make the temple a priority in your given circumstances. As you make temple worship a part of your life, expect opposition from the enemy of your soul; he understands the power that comes from regular temple service. You have the power to choose and overcome his distractions.[84] Choose to reconnect with heaven.

If a temple is close to where you live, you can consider the opportunity to go once a week if you so choose. I, and many others,

---

[82] *Preparing to Enter the Holy Temple*, (2002), 1-37.
[83] "LDS Temple Open House Reservations," *templeopenhouse.lds.org* (accessed May 7, 2016).
[84] 2 Nephi 2:27.

have learned that it is a lot easier to go once a week than once a month. There is nothing to explain it; it just is. Put it to the test to see if a tangible difference is felt in your life. [85] Remember Doctrine and Covenants 82:3: "For of him unto whom much is given much is required." It can be so easy to take the temple for granted, but we cannot do that! The power of the temple can be a steady enabling gift in our lives, if we so choose. I always say that the temple is not an *escape from* reality; the temple *is* reality.

The people I taught in Southern Argentina do not currently have any temples close to their proximity. It is something they yearn for, and something I still pray for on their behalf. I saw many people make great sacrifices to be able to go to one of the nearest temples. Of the two closest temples one was over 700 miles away, and the other was in a completely different country. I know there are many people in this world that have temples even further from their homes, and their desires to attend the House of the Lord and their sacrifices to make that a reality are heroic in my eyes.

When these individuals get the rare, blessed, and sometimes once in a lifetime opportunity for the temple to be their Sacred Time moment of the day, they do not take it for granted. The apostle, Richard G. Scott, reminded us:

> I have seen that many times individuals have made great sacrifices to go to a distant temple. But when a temple is built close by, within a short time, many do not visit it regularly…When a temple is conveniently nearby, small things may interrupt your plans to go to the temple. Set specific goals, considering your circumstances, of when you can and will participate in temple ordinances. Then do not allow anything to interfere with that plan.[86]

---

[85] Isaiah 55:8-9.
[86] Richard G. Scott, "Temple Worship: The Source of Strength and Power in Times of Need," *Ensign*, May 2009, 43-45.

I have friends and loved ones who once partook of the joys of frequent temple worship and, with time, have chosen to forget and neglect their covenants. Does the Lord say, "Sorry, you messed up, see ya never!"? No!! Repeatedly we are taught from the Lord's prophets and the Lord Himself:

> *Will ye not now return unto me,* and repent of your sins, and be converted, that I may heal you? Yea, verily I say unto you, if ye will come unto me ye shall have eternal life. Behold, mine arm of mercy is extended towards you, and whosoever will come, him will I receive; and blessed are those who come unto me.[87]

Any thought that communicates that it is too late to return to Christ's path or that coming back to Christ's fold will be too hard, too embarrassing, or too time-consuming is a self-destructive belief that is directly linked to lies from Satan. The devil knows that the blessings found within Christ's church and temples can allow for godly growth. The beloved prophet, Thomas S. Monson, has said:

> I think there is no place in the world where I feel closer to the Lord than in one of His holy temples. As we go to the holy house, as we remember the covenants we make therein, we will be able to bear every trial and overcome each temptation. The temple provides purpose for our lives. It brings peace to our souls—not the peace provided by men but the peace promised by [Jesus Christ] when He said, "Peace I leave with you, my peace I give unto you: not as the world giveth, give I unto you. Let not your heart be troubled, neither let it be afraid."[88]

I know from personal experience that temple worship is one of the most sublime blessings in our lives. It is also one of the most

---

[87] 3 Nephi 9:13-14; emphasis added.
[88] Thomas S. Monson, "Blessings of the Temple," *Ensign*, Oct. 2010, *lds.org* (accessed May 1. 2016); see John 14:27.

wonderful and important Sacred Time Star opportunities we have. Whatever spiritual state we are in, let us raise the bar in terms of our opportunities for temple worship. *Reconnect and Remember.*

Sacred Time Star Everyday

In order to have a full 5 Star Day, each Star needs to be a daily occurrence, right? Clearly I cannot go to the temple and to church every single day. What additional activities can I do in order to fulfill my Sacred Time Star? Truth be told, sometimes my Sacred Time Star need not be any longer than a few minutes. That is part of the reason why I sometimes refer to this Star as a Sacred Time *moment.*

This Star used to be called the Sacred Grove Star. This is in reference to the grove where the prophet Joseph Smith went to be away from worldly noise to ask God which of all the churches were true. This prayer was significant, and because he chose to separate himself in a quiet place he was able to receive the answer to his prayer. We too have a need to make the effort to reconnect with heaven daily, and this reconnection takes place as we make the choice to briefly get away from the noise of the world. Although this Star is no longer called the Sacred Grove Star, the divine principle of finding time to reconnect with heaven still applies.

Again, the other Stars in the 5 Star Day are cleansing and sacred as well. However, there is something very powerful about the choice to do a *very specific act* daily that puts us in a holy state of mind away from the noise and distractions in our lives. We are then blessed with enhanced ability to be still in holy places and Remember.

The Savior often spent time to pause and be away from the world, gaining help and guidance from Heavenly Father.[89] Elder Richard G. Scott taught:

---

[89] Mark 1:35; Luke 5:16; Luke 6:12; Matthew 14:13.

> [Guidance and answer to prayer] will seldom come as the prayer is offered, rather in quiet moments when the Spirit can most effectively touch your mind and heart. Hence the need for periods of quiet time to keep perspective and to be instructed and strengthened.[90]

In addition to what we have discussed about temple and church worship, other super important Sacred Time experiences include: *family history work* (we will talk about that in a moment), *reviewing our patriarchal blessings* (personal counsel from the Lord for your life), *institute and seminary* (classes given locally that teach of Christ and His gospel), and *family home evening* (an evening set aside weekly to be together as a family, to have a short gospel lesson, and to do something fun together).[91] I feel to add the importance of having a *regular date night with your spouse* that is focused on edifying each other and Remembering. [92] These Sacred Time activities should be incorporated accordingly. The Lord encourages them all. As noted before, any sacred activity does not automatically constitute for a Sacred Time moment—that connection takes effort on our part.

There are many other Sacred Time places and activities. These come in a grand variety, and they vary from person to person. Your job is to find a plethora of options that work for you that allow for you to be still, stand in holy places, and Remember.

Examples include: going for a walk with the intent to refocus on eternal truths, drawing a picture, appreciating pictures of Christ while listening to your favorite hymn, participating in yoga and meditation with deep breathing, taking in the beauty of nature on a hike, playing the piano, journal keeping, knitting, etc.

Whatever be your individualized Sacred Time moment of the day, make it count. Again, focus on quality rather than quantity.

---

[90] Richard G. Scott, "Making the Right Choices," Jan. 2002, *speeches.byu.edu* (accessed March 23, 2017).

[91] "Patriarchal Blessings," *lds.org*; "Seminary and Institute," *lds.org*; "Family Home Evening," *lds.org*.

[92] Douglas Brinley, "What Happily Married Couples Do," *Ensign*, Jan. 2012, 12-14; Lynn G. Robbins, "Agency and Love in Marriage," *Ensign*, Oct. 2000, *lds.org* (accessed Aug. 22, 2017).

Example 1

My sister, Janessa, was a high-achieving, busy nursing student at BYU-Idaho. She also frequently had many activities and callings that invested portions of her time. It was during that time that she began to experience the beginnings of what she called a 5 Star Day. She acknowledged the necessity of scripture study, sincere prayer, and service. She also recognized the words of the prophets in relation to Sacred Time moments and places. She pondered on what she could do to have a specific activity to help her get away from the world for a few minutes to just reconnect with heaven and Remember.

She found that, for her personality and needs, going on campus once a day to play hymns on a piano in an empty classroom allowed greater peace and strength to come to her. It was like the frosting that combined all the layers of her good efforts from the other Stars and made them even sweeter. This allowed her time to "regroup" and feel God's love.

There were many days in which setting her cell phone and to-do list aside and sitting at that sacred piano was what kept her moving forward and allowed for the gift of Remembrance. The small piano room became her Sacred Grove. It was her place to be still, stand in a holy place, refocus, and Remember. She did not need hours of time, just a few minutes. *Reconnect and Remember.*

Example 2

I have been involved in athletics since I was a little girl and when I reached high school I was prompted by the Spirit—and persuaded by some great friends—to switch from soccer to cross country.

Sincerely, it was one of the best decisions of my life. God knew what life lessons I needed to learn and what friendships I needed to deepen by running on the cross country team. Life lessons of hard work, endurance, teamwork, and many other things were engrained upon my soul. I did not necessarily like running, but I loved how I felt doing hard things with true friends.

Since that time in my life, I have needed a new motivation to keep me in the running habit. As I embarked the path of adulthood, I began jogging for the mere opportunity to get away from the stresses of the day. In high school I listened to music whenever I ran alone, but with time I decided to disconnect from my cell phone and my earphones—other than listening to an occasional talk from General Conference. I ran to be in touch with the beauties of nature around me, have time to think, enjoy moments to refocus, and savor the ability to ponder.

Jogging is still one of my cherished Sacred Time moments, when my schedule and the weather permit. I feel a solidifying of the scripture study, prayer, and service I strive for, and I have gotten to the point that I look forward to the time I can take a breather, be in nature, commune with the Lord, and just Remember.

Reconnect and Remember.

Example 3

I have many family members—especially Janessa—and friends who have relayed the power that journal writing has had in their lives as their Sacred Time moment of the day.

From the leaders of the church and the Lord Himself, journal writing has always been encouraged as a way to fulfill the Sacred Time Star.[93] It helps us focus on blessings in our lives from the present and the past. President Eyring told this story about journal keeping and useful tools that helped him get into the habit:

> Before I would write, I would ponder this question: "Have I seen the hand of God reaching out to touch [me] or [my] family today?" As I kept at it, something began to

---

[93] "President Kimball Speaks Out on Personal Journals," *Ensign*, July 2014, *lds.org* (accessed Dec. 20, 2016); see 3 Nephi 23:7-14; 2 Nephi 25:23&26; 2 Nephi 33:2-3; Exodus 24:4.

happen. As I would cast my mind over the day, I would see evidence of what God had done for [us] that I had not recognized in the busy moments of the day. As that happened, and it happened often, I realized that trying to remember had allowed God to show me what He had done.[94]

When days are just plain old hard, and the clouds of gloom seem unremitting, Sister Carole M. Stevens encourages us to Remember the Lord's hand in our lives from the past. She taught that we can "rely on the memory of His tender mercies. They [can] serve as a guiding light as [we] navigate through hard times."[95]

Consistent journal keeping allows for healing to our souls and can help us stay on the Lord's path. This comment by Elder Ronald A. Rasband confirms the power that comes from journal keeping:

> Generations are affected by the choices we make. Share your testimony with your family…remember how [you] felt when [you] recognized the Spirit in [your life] and…record those feelings in journals and personal histories so that [your] own words may, when needed, bring to [your] remembrance how good the Lord has been to [you].[96]

I love those thoughts. I have experienced great strength and an enhanced ability to Remember and recognize the Lord's hand in my life when I am consistent with my journal writing.

Through regular emails, my parents write about tender mercies and the ways they have seen the hand of God in their lives and in our family. These simple emails help our family stay connected as we are living in different parts of the nation, and they also give us an enhanced gift to see the miracles around us. *Reconnect and Remember.*

---

[94] Henry B. Eyring, "O Remember, Remember," *Ensign*, Nov. 2007, 66-69.
[95] Carole M. Stevens, "The Master Healer," *Ensign*, Nov. 2016, 9-11.
[96] Ronald A. Rasband, "Lest Thou Forget," *Ensign*, Nov. 2016, 113-115; see Deuteronomy 4:9.

<u>Example 4</u>

I have experienced another powerful option for the Sacred Time Star. It is searching for the names and information of our ancestors who have passed away without the saving ordinances of the gospel. Saving ordinances are the steps to return home and the application of the Savior's Atonement (see <u>Chapter 2</u>).

We can take their names to the temple and do saving ordinances on their behalf like: baptism, obtaining the gift of the Holy Ghost, receiving one's endowment, and being sealed to one's family.

In the spirit world, our ancestors have the opportunity to accept or reject those ordinances. It is important to note that little children who have passed away—having died in pure innocence without baptism—will be saved in the kingdom of God.[97] The Lord is kind. If someone did not get the chance to take those vital steps to return home while on the earth, they will be given the opportunity to accept the gospel on the other side.[98] This is still their choice.

The deep importance of doing temple work for our ancestors is summed up wonderfully in Doctrine and Covenants 128:18: "For we without them cannot be made perfect; neither can they without us be made perfect." This is a marvelous work!

Elder Richard G. Scott, of the Quorum of the Twelve Apostles, said, in regards to participating in family history and temple work, "I can think of no greater protection from the influence of the adversary in your life."[99] Considering the world that we live in, this is no small thing. We all need protection from the evil influences surrounding us.

Touching on this matter, I have learned to pay attention when apostles of the Lord make a promise. Referring to family history and

---

[97] Moroni 8:5-10.
[98] 1 Peter 3:18-19; *Doctrine and Covenants* 138:58-59; Malachi 4:6.
[99] Richard G. Scott, "The Joy of Redeeming the Dead," *Ensign*, Nov. 2012, 94.

temple work, Elder David A. Bednar and Elder Richard G. Scott *promised* the following blessings from the Lord:

- Your conversion to the Savior will become deeper.
- You will receive light and knowledge through the Holy Ghost.
- Your testimony will be strengthened.
- Your patriarchal blessing will become more meaningful.
- Your love and gratitude for your ancestors will grow.
- You will have greater opportunities to serve.
- Your service in the temple will become more sacred.[100]

Wow. How different would our lives be if we personally and as a family enjoyed these promises? Family history work is wonderful; I cannot think of a better way to use our cell phones and the internet. I know these promised blessings above are real. I have felt divine protection from the adversary while finding and learning about my ancestors and performing temple work on their behalf. I encourage you to put the Lord to the test. As we do our part to experiment upon the guidance He gives us through His chosen prophets and apostles, we can come to know that the words they speak and promises they give are indeed from God. *Reconnect and Remember.*

Example 5

The Sacred Time Star is important in times of ease and as well as times of hardship. Elder L. Tom Perry would disconnect from worldly noise during a difficult time in his life:

> We drove to a place just a few miles from our home to get away for a few moments of relief from our troubles, talk, and give emotional comfort to each other. Our place was Walden Pond. It was a beautiful...pond surrounded

---

[100] "Simple Steps to Find Powerful Spiritual Protection," *lds.org/youth* (accessed Nov. 20, 2016).

by forests of trees. Walden Pond was our special place to pause, reflect, and heal.[101]

President Henry B. Eyring taught:

> We each promise to remember the Savior. You can choose to remember Him in the way that best draws your heart to Him. Sometimes for me, it is to see Him in my mind kneeling in the Garden of Gethsemane or to see Him calling Lazarus to come forth from the tomb. As I do, I feel a closeness to Him and a gratitude that brings peace to my heart.[102]

There are some heavy things we may be called to pass through in our mortal lives. Perhaps there are times in which we feel the Lord has forgotten us. Isaiah does not mince the Lord's words in His very powerful messianic declaration:

> But Zion said, The Lord hath forsaken me, and my Lord hath forgotten me. Can a woman forget her sucking child, that she should not have compassion on the son of her womb? Yea, they may forget, yet will I not forget thee. Behold, I have graven thee upon the palms of my hands.[103]

Though there are times that we may feel the Lord is far away or that He has forgotten us, He hasn't. The powerful reality that we are symbolically and literally engraved on the palms of His hands gives us light on just how much the Lord is aware of us. He is the King of the word Remember. As we take small moments to *reconnect with heaven and Remember* Him daily, we will find strength.

Example 6

The possibilities are seemingly endless. I feel to share three other opportunities for potential Sacred Time moments.

---

[101] L. Tom Perry, "Let Him Do It With Simplicity," *Ensign*, Nov. 2008, 7-10.
[102] Henry B. Eyring, "Peace in This Life," *Ensign*, Dec. 2016, 4-5.
[103] Isaiah 49:14-16.

First, Elder F. Enzio Busche gave a powerful talk to the students at Brigham Young University. Highlights of these insights are found in a six minute YouTube video.[104] If you are ever struggling to think of a simple way to fulfil the Sacred Time Star of the day, I encourage you to watch this YouTube video and really pay attention to the words shared. Elder Busche gives us enhanced perspective on life and simple teachings that can bring light and peace to each of us.

Second, music can have a great influence in our lives—for good or for bad. It can be a great resource for reconnecting with heaven and Remembering. Music that invites the Holy Spirit also invites revelation. Some of the most holy experiences of my life have been directly connected with music. May each of us utilize this divine gift.

Lastly, I had the thought to share the wisdom in participating in a Sacred Time event at least once a year. This is not required, but it can be beneficial. Some Sacred Time events could include: being a part of a spiritual youth camp, making the temple the focus of a vacation, participating in Girl's Camp/Scout Camp or the Trek, enjoying an inspiring pageant about Christ, doing a church history tour, having a day in nature, etc. It can be strengthening to plan for a yearly Sacred Time event that helps us *reconnect and Remember.*

Important Reminder

Apart from going to church and to the temple, I think I neglect the Sacred Time Star the most often of all the Stars. I feel a tangible difference in my life when I reapply it consistently. This Star helps us recognize the Lord's hand in our lives and truly Remember.

Once while I was in a yoga class, the instructor encouraged us to take ten minutes a day "to slow down" and "to do nothing." She promised that those ten minutes spent away (i.e. spent reconnecting with heaven and Remembering) would accumulate into even more

---

[104] "Advice from Elder Busche," *youtube.com*; (accessed Jan 1, 2016).

than ten minutes of productivity added to our day. I accepted her challenge and allowed the experience to be my Sacred Time moment of the day. When not at church or in the temple, this can be a great tool for reconnecting and Remembering during the week. This activity is a very good option to keep in mind.

I decided to share with you four examples of Sacred Time moments that we might choose throughout any given week. These examples are not given with the intention for you to strictly follow them; rather, they are given to show some idea of how we can enjoy Sacred Time moments every day throughout the week. With all of these examples, there can be great benefit in consistently choosing to turn off our cell phones during the Sacred Time Star. You can enjoy the Sacred Time Star daily as you find places and activities that help you personally reconnect with heaven and Remember.

Example 1:

- Sunday: Partake of sacrament/church worship (vital).
- Monday: Family Home Evening (vital).
- Tuesday: Go for a walk outside; focus on the beauties of the earth.
- Wednesday: Play hymns on the piano; pay attention to the words.
- Thursday: Find one family name to take to the temple.
- Friday: Go to the temple (regular attendance is vital).
- Saturday: Write in my journal the ways that I saw God's hand in my life this week.

Example 2

- Sunday: Partake of sacrament/church worship (vital).
- Monday: Family Home Evening (vital).
- Tuesday: Close eyes and breathe deeply while listening to a favorite hymn/inspiring song.

- Wednesday: Go for a walk or jog while enjoying nature.
- Thursday: Attend an Institute class.
- Friday: Have an edifying date night with your spouse (vital for married folks).
- Saturday: Refocus and think of the Savior while drawing a picture.

Example 3:

- Sunday: Partake of sacrament/church worship (vital).
- Monday: Singles Ward Family Home Evening (important).
- Tuesday: Review Five Unchanging Truths while looking at a picture of the temple (these truths will be taught in the next chapter).
- Wednesday: Swim while refocusing on life's purpose.
- Thursday: Play hymns on the violin.
- Friday: Sit on the patio, and enjoy the sunset.
- Saturday: Go fishing; think of the Savior.

Example 4:

- Sunday: If at work, go on lunch break to a nearby church building to partake of the sacrament; enjoy church music.
- Monday: Attend Ward Family Night (important).
- Tuesday: Study patriarchal blessing.
- Wednesday: Think of Christ while cleaning the house (and how He helps keep our spirits clean) with uplifting music.
- Thursday: Watch the youtube video by Elder Busche.
- Friday: Look at pictures from a spiritually significant event in the past (options: Girl's/Scout Camp, EFY photos, missionary album, wedding pictures, baptism day, etc.). Remember how you felt during that Sacred Time event.
- Saturday: Sit on temple grounds and ponder moments from the Savior's life.

Make It a 5 Star Day!

✳ ✳ ✳ ✳ ✳

Amidst the busyness of life and the day-to-day noise, may you and I choose to reconnect with heaven, slow down, be still, and Remember. As we continue to stand in holy places—especially the church and the temple—we can live in a state of holiness. Oh how the adversary would love for us to neglect this Star, and oh how he strives to keep us from being still and from choosing to maximize our experiences in holy places. We have power to choose. God will always Remember us; may we choose daily to reconnect with and Remember Him. I have felt the influence and sustaining strength that comes into my life when I choose to consistently apply the Sacred Time Star. It truly changes everything. *Reconnect and Remember.*

Chapter 8

5 Star Day:

Smile

IN MY PERSPECTIVE, one of the greatest physical features that can be had by a human being is the feature of smile wrinkles by the eyes. In my mind's eye, I can see clear as day the faces of certain individuals I have met that have those amazing smile lines! And now that I think of it, those people smiled a lot (surprise!). Smiling is powerful. I like to think of smiling as a reflection of the heart.

Is the Smile Star implying solely the physical smile on our faces? If we do not have smile lines, are we failures at the Smile Star? Does it mean that we have to walk around with pearly whites so big that it makes us say, "My cheeks are killing me!"? Thank you Tour Guide Barbie (Toy Story 2). The answer is no!

The truth is there are ups and downs in our mortal journey. We can have phases in our lives when smiling is natural and abundant. On the other hand, there may be times when we have no desire to smile. There is opposition in all things.[1] It is ok to feel frustrated, sad, lonely, or upset at times. These emotions are a part of life. Though many of life's situations may be out of our hands, the Lord

---

[1] 2 Nephi 2:11.

has given us the power to *choose* how to respond, adjust, press forward, and keep smiling.[2]

Like the rest of the Stars in a 5 Star Day, the Smile Star is more about the condition of the heart.[3] The underlying foundation of the Smile Star is made up of these two principles: gratitude and joy. These two gifts bring the beauties of the world and the beauties of our lives into focus.

In relation to this subject, I am going to share the first and last verses of the song *For the Beauty of the Earth*. Please do not just skim over the words. Really think about the divine message of this hymn. The lyrics of this beloved hymn have the power to uplift our hearts as we Remember the bounteous blessings from the Lord and His love for us.

For the beauty of the earth,
For the beauty of the skies,
For the love which from our birth
Over and around us lies,
Lord of all, to thee we raise
This our hymn of grateful praise.

For the joy of human love,
Brother, sister, parent, child,
Friends on earth, and friends above,
For all gentle thoughts and mild,
Lord of all, to thee we raise
This our hymn of grateful praise.[4]

As children of God, we have a lot to be grateful for. When times are tough, I usually need to choose to see the world from a higher view.

---

[2] Thomas S. Monson, "Living the Abundant Life," *Ensign*, Jan. 2012, 4-5.
[3] Virginia H. Pearce, *A Heart Like His*, April 2002.
[4] "For the Beauty of the Earth," *Hymns*, no. 92.

The amazing thing about applying gratitude to every aspect of our lives and choosing to smile daily is that smiling does not only take an effect on our own personal joy but the joy of others.

Elder Hugo Montoya related the experiences he had with the power of smiling when he had recently been called to be a General Authority (general leader of Christ's church world-wide):

> [The] small action [of smiling] can help those who are overwhelmed or burdened. During the priesthood session of this past April general conference, I was seated on the stand as one of the five newly called General Authorities...I was feeling very nervous and overwhelmed with my new call.
>
> When we were singing the intermediate hymn, I felt a strong impression that someone was watching me. While I continued singing, I again felt the strong impression that someone was watching me. I looked over to the row where the Twelve Apostles were sitting and saw that President Russell M. Nelson was turned all the way around in his seat, looking at where we were seated. I caught his eye, and he gave me a big smile. That smile brought peace to my overwhelmed heart.
>
> After His Resurrection, Jesus Christ visited His other sheep. He called and ordained twelve disciples, and with that authority, they ministered to the people. The Lord Jesus Christ Himself stood among them. The Lord asked them to kneel and pray.
>
> I am not sure if the newly called and ordained twelve disciples were overwhelmed with their calling, but the scripture says, "It came to pass that Jesus blessed them as they did pray unto him; and his countenance did smile upon them."[5]

5 Hugo Montoya, "Tested and Tempted---but Helped," *Ensign*, Nov. 2015, 53-55; see 3 Nephi 19:25.

There have been many times in my life when I have felt a boost and tangible comfort when someone takes the time to smile at me. Through the ups and downs of life, smiling can be a healing balm.

The Black Dot

Our lives are continually changing. With every transition stage in life there are always good things and bad things. From there, we get to choose what to focus on.

As a mental health professional, I often times teach my patients through visual learning. There is a significant object lesson that was taught to me by my first mission president's wife, Brenda. I share this lesson regularly with my patients.

To start, I grab a white sheet of paper and I color a nickel-sized black dot somewhere on the page. The paper is shown to my patient and I ask, "What do you see?"

Most of the time the individual points out facts about the black dot: location, darkness, size, awkwardness on the page, etc. Their interpretations are not wrong; I assure them of that. They are then encouraged to see the paper from a different perspective.

I pose the question: "How much white is on the page compared to the black dot?" The individual typically sits back and then relays that the white on the paper is far greater than the black dot.

I teach them that we each have struggles and turmoil at literally every phase of life. These times can be likened unto the "black dot." The black dots, or conflicts, are diverse with each new phase but are present. Challenges help us grow and learn, and they can be really difficult sometimes!!

Through the hardships there is still good in this world and there are still good things in our lives! If we focus solely on the "black dots" in our lives, we miss out on the "white" surrounding us. As we diligently train our minds and hearts to magnify the white, the black dot does not necessarily go away; rather, we are in a position to "act" and not let our circumstances "[act] upon" us.[6] This is the power of gratitude. President Thomas S. Monson taught:

> It would be easy to become discouraged and cynical...if we allowed ourselves to dwell only on that which is wrong in the world and in our lives. [We must] turn our thoughts and our attitudes away from the troubles around us and... focus instead on our blessings. "Wherefore, be of good cheer, and do not fear, for I the Lord am with you, and will stand by you."[7]

Truly Jesus Christ is the unchanging "white" in our lives. That reality in itself can give us strength to keep striving and keep smiling.

Again, I have done this exercise with many different patients in the mental health field. Their struggles are not easy. I have witnessed time and time again as they make the constant effort to fill their perspective with the "white" in their lives they are given help from on high and granted the promise that Christ "will console you in your afflictions," and will be "[your] strength."[8] Whether the patient believes in God or not, His divine help is felt. Gratitude is powerful.

Often times, the black dot can become a part of the white in our lives as we learn, grow, and realize that the Lord was guiding us all along. Elder Joe J. Christensen acknowledged this:

> There are times...when things are so overwhelming that it is challenging to feel gratitude. We all face difficulties at some time or another, and occasionally they are [very] tough. But in every case, you probably find out later that there was something the Lord was teaching us, something that is or will be of immense importance in our lives.[9]

---

[6] 2 Nephi 2:26; *Doctrine and Covenants* 123:17.
[7] Thomas S. Monson, "Be of Good Cheer," *Ensign*, May 2009, 89-92.
[8] Jacob 3:1; Exodus 15:2; Job 12:13; Mosiah 9:17.
[9] Joe J. Christensen, "A Reason to Smile," *Ensign*, February 2002, *lds.org* (accessed June 18, 2016).

Speaking of black dots, since the beginning of this world all have passed through trials and tribulations. Let's talk about the very first people to walk the earth: Adam and Eve. They did not only bear the death of their righteous son, Abel, but they were allotted the trial of their eldest son, Cain, being the one who chose to kill him.[10]

Abraham, Isaac, Jacob, Abinadi, Joseph Smith, Moses, Alma, Nephi, Enoch, John the Baptist, Peter, Paul—I could go on and on through all generations of time—all passed through intense afflictions. Above all, the Savior was called "a man of sorrows, acquainted with grief."[11] When Jesus Christ suffered for our sins and afflictions, He "descended below all things" and suffered "temptations, and pain of body, hunger, thirst, and fatigue, even more than man can suffer, except it be unto death; for behold, blood [came] from every pore, so great [was His] anguish…for [His] people."[12] Wow…what remarkable love.

A common thread among all these individuals is that they did not give up! We are to "run with patience the race that is set before us."[13] We are each walking our own individual paths that allow for our optimal eternal growth. Like Paul, may we be able to say, "I have fought a good fight, I have finished my course, I have kept my faith."[14] My friend, Robert, has noted, "Many of the most righteous people, especially Christ, suffered numerous trials and heartaches. However, with the heartache and trials they also received many blessings. I think a lot of people wonder why they have trials if they are keeping the commandments. I think unique challenges are given to each of us so we can overcome them, trust in God, and become more like Him as we go through life." The Lord wants us to walk our individual paths with trust that He has our best interest in mind.

---

[10] Moses 5:17; Genesis 4:2-4.

[11] Mosiah 14:3.

[12] *Doctrine and Covenants* 88:6; *Doctrine and Covenants* 122; Mosiah 3:7; *Doctrine and Covenants* 19:18.

[13] Hebrews 12:1.

[14] 2 Timothy 4:7.

My friend, Caitlyn, once said in a testimony meeting, "In tough times, the most healing action is to choose to remember the Savior. Why do I complain when my life is not a rose garden when He wore the crown of thorns?" Al Carroway, a motivational speaker who has been through many intense trials in her life, said, "Hard times will always be there, but so will Christ." [15] The prophet, Thomas S. Monson, powerfully taught:

> Our Heavenly Father, who gives us so much to delight in, also knows that we learn and grow and become stronger as we face and survive the trials through which we must pass. We know that there are times when we will experience heartbreaking sorrow, when we will grieve, and when we may be tested to our limits. However, such difficulties allow us to change for the better, to rebuild our lives in the way our Heavenly Father teaches us, and to become something different from what we were—better than we were, more understanding than we were, more empathetic than we were, with stronger testimonies than we had before.
>
> This should be our purpose—to persevere and endure, yes, but also to become more spiritually refined as we make our way through sunshine and sorrow. Were it not for challenges to overcome and problems to solve, we would remain much as we are, with little or no progress toward our goal of eternal life. [16]

We are here on earth to change and experience transformation through Christ's Atonement. Truly, trials can help us come to know Christ, become more like Him, and help us gain divine compassion for others. If we take any trial and put Christ next to it, all of a sudden the affliction seems a lot easier to endure.

Do you remember the last step taught in the gospel of Jesus Christ (the steps to return home in Chapter 2)? The last process is

---

[15] Al Fox Carroway, *More Than the Tattooed Mormon*, Nov. 2015.
[16] Thomas S. Monson, "I Will Not Fail Thee, nor Forsake Thee," *Ensign*, Nov. 2013, 85-87.

what the Lord calls "enduring to the end."[17] Of all the steps to return home, this is the finishing touch. It is a crucial transformation step. It includes continually retaking the other steps as well as inviting others to take these steps.[18] Christ is the perfect example of this.[19] He did not give up, and He did not fail us.

Robert D. Hales reminded us, "We were not sent by Father in Heaven just to be born. We were sent to endure and return to Him with honor."[20] The scriptures teach: "Behold, we count them happy which endure."[21] This is the future for those who have persevered: "The redeemed of the Lord shall return, and come with singing unto Zion; and everlasting joy and holiness shall be upon their heads; and they shall obtain gladness and joy; sorrow and mourning shall flee away."[22]

Wow. I want to be there. Living with God again will be so worth it.[23] I know that as we ask for Christ's help, we can focus on the white in our lives and we can press forward.

Gratitude and Joy

The modern-day apostle, Russell M. Nelson, has experienced many hardships. These struggles have included: the responsibilities of being a cardiac surgeon, pressing forward after the death of his wife, and the heart ache of losing his daughter to cancer. Yet, he bore testimony and promised, "When the focus of our lives is on Jesus Christ and His gospel, we can feel joy regardless of what is happening—or not happening—in our lives."[24] What hope!

---

[17] Matthew 10:22; 1 Nephi 13:37; Alma 5:13; *Doctrine and Covenants* 121:29; 2 Nephi 31:20.

[18] 2 Nephi 31:19-21; Omni 1:26; John 21:15-17; *Doctrine and Covenants* 4:1-7; Helaman 3:35; Alma 5:13.

[19] John 6:38; John 5:30; Luke 22:42; John 19:30; Mosiah 15:1-7.

[20] Robert D. Hales, "Behold, We Count Them Happy Which Endure," *Ensign*, May 1998, *lds.org*, The Church of Jesus Christ of Latter-day Saints, May 1998 (accessed Nov. 8, 2016).

[21] James 5:11.

[22] 2 Nephi 8:11.

[23] 2 Nephi 8:11; 2 Nephi 9:18; *Doctrine and Covenants* 131:1-4; John 17:3; Alma 5:57.

[24] Russell M. Nelson, "Joy and Spiritual Survival," *Ensign*, Nov. 2016, 81-84.

President Nelson emphasized that joy is "key to our spiritual survival."[25] That is part of why the Smile Star is essential in order to keep moving forward in life. In fact, the divine necessity for joy is not just a passive need but is the very purpose of our existence. The scriptures teach that "men are, that they might have joy."[26] President Nelson continued, "Saints can be happy under every circumstance. We can feel joy even while having a bad day, a bad week, or even a bad year! The joy we feel has little to do with the *circumstances* of our lives and everything to do with the *focus* of our lives."[27] So how do we obtain this joy? He went on to name the two key teachings we need to focus on in order to acquire Christ's joy:

1. God's Plan of Salvation (Chapter 2 of this book).
2. Jesus Christ and His gospel (Chapter 2 steps to return home).

President Nelson spoke of Christ as he taught:

> He is the source of all joy... it doesn't seem possible to feel joy when your child suffers with an incurable illness or when you lose your job or when your spouse betrays you. Yet that is precisely the joy the Savior offers. His joy is constant, assuring us that our "afflictions shall be but a small moment" and be consecrated to our gain.[28]

President Nelson gave five more helpful guides for feeling joy:

- *Give thanks* to God in our prayers.
- Keep and renew the *covenants* we have made with Him.
- *Ask for His joy* to be felt and given unto us.
- *Avoid things that can interrupt our joy*, or in other words, anything that opposes Christ or His doctrine.
- *Choose Heavenly Father to be our God.*[29]

---

[25] Russell M. Nelson, "Joy and Spiritual Survival," *Ensign*, Nov. 2016, 81-84.
[26] 2 Nephi 2:25; John 16:33.
[27] Russell M. Nelson, "Joy and Spiritual Survival," *Ensign*, Nov. 2016, 81-84
[28] Russell M. Nelson, "Joy and Spiritual Survival," *Ensign*, Nov. 2016, 81-84; *Doctrine and Covenants* 121:7; 2 Nephi 2:2.
[29] Russell M. Nelson, "Joy and Spiritual Survival," *Ensign*, Nov. 2016, 81-84; emphasis added.

Elder Jeffrey R. Holland also helped us understand how we can live after the manner of happiness even while having black dots (or hard circumstances) in our lives. Please read what he said slowly and with an open heart. Pay attention to what the Spirit teaches you:

> Learn as quickly as you can that so much of your happiness is in your hands. In anticipation of giving this talk, I sat in my study for a long time trying to think if I had ever known a happy person who was unkind or unpleasant to be with. And guess what? I couldn't think of one, not a single, solitary one. Happy people aren't negative or cynical or mean so don't plan on that being part of the "manner" of happiness. If my life has taught me anything, it is that kindness and pleasantness and faith-based optimism are characteristics of happy people.
>
> *In short, your best chance for being happy is to do the things that happy people do.* Live the way happy people live. Walk the path that happy people walk…Your chances to find joy in unexpected moments, to find peace in unexpected places, to find the help of angels when you didn't even know they knew you existed, improves exponentially.
>
> Ultimate happiness, true peace, and anything even remotely close to joy are found first, foremost, and forever in *living the gospel of Jesus Christ.* Lots of other philosophies and systems of belief have been tried. Indeed it seems safe to say that virtually every other philosophy and system has been tried down through the centuries of history…the prophet David O. McKay [taught], "[Unlike gratification or pleasure or some kind of thrill, true] happiness is found *only* along that well beaten [gospel] track, narrow as it is,…[and] straight [as it is], which leads to life eternal." So love God and each other, and be true to the gospel of Jesus Christ.[30]

---

30 Jeffrey R. Holland, "Living After the Manner of Happiness," Sep. 2014, *www2.byui.edu* (accessed March 28, 3017); emphasis added; see 2 Nephi 5:27.

I know that it can be tough to have an attitude of gratitude and to feel Christ's joy during severe challenges. However, I know that we can do it. When we choose gratitude and joy to fill our views, the Smile Star becomes a beacon in our lives that brightens all the other Stars. Elder Nelson continued: "Joy is a gift for the faithful. It is the gift that comes from intentionally trying to live a righteous life, as taught by Jesus Christ."[31]

We cannot live in a state of joy if we are choosing to live in sin and rebel against God.[32] We may still experience temporary pleasure, but it will be fleeting because we are living contrary to the state of happiness.[33] An extremely important part of feeling Christ's joy is the process of repentance. We are all in this important process.

The Joy of Repentance

One of the essential steps to return home is continual, daily repentance. When we do anything that is contrary to the loving commandments of God (i.e. when we sin), this makes us "unclean" before God. Remember that no "unclean thing" can dwell in His presence.[34] Through the Atonement of Jesus Christ we can become clean and whole again. Faith and repentance are the first two steps.

We must start by having faith in Christ and truly believing Him when He said, "I am the light of the world: he that followeth me shall not walk in darkness, but shall have the light of life."[35] True faith requires action.[36] He is our Savior, and He paid the crucial price for us to receive a remission of our sins (forgiveness). We must also choose to believe Christ when He said, "Behold, he who has repented of his sins, the same is forgiven, and I, the Lord,

---

[31] Russell M. Nelson, "Joy and Spiritual Survival," *Ensign*, Nov. 2016, 81-84.
[32] Alma 41:10; Alma 41:3; Mormon 2:12-14; John 13:14-17; James 4:8-10.
[33] Alma 41:11; Alma 41:3; Alma 41:10.
[34] 1 Nephi 10:21; Romans 3:23; 2 Nephi 2:15-16; 1 Kings 8:46; 1 John 3:4.
[35] John 8:12.
[36] James 2:17-26; Alma 32:21; Ether 4:12; Ether 12:4-9; Hebrews 11; Alma 32:40-43.

remember [their sins] no more."[37] As we act upon His teachings and truly follow Him, our faith increases.

This faith and action leads us to repent of our sins. Repentance denotes a "change of mind, a fresh view about God, about oneself, and about the world."[38] Repentance is godly change. This entails becoming a little better day-by-day, choosing to forsake (or let go of) sin, and making amends for the wrongs we have done. [39] *Repentance is joyful.* The Saviors wants to forgive us. Elder Jeffrey R. Holland taught:

> However late you think you are, however many chances you think you have missed, however many mistakes you feel you have made or talents you think you don't have, or however far from home and family and God you feel you have traveled, I testify that you have not traveled beyond the reach of divine love. It is not possible for you to sink lower than the infinite light of Christ's Atonement shines.[40]

Repentance can be hard but it is joyful. The responsibility is ours to utilize this divine gift. [41] New beginnings are real, and godly transformation is a promise to those who come unto Him.[42] Daily repentance makes all the difference in this life and after we die.

Our State of Joy After This Life

One of the most glorious and hopeful truths in all of scripture is this: the resurrection. After Christ's suffering in the garden of Gethsemane and agony and death on the cross, His crucified body was laid in a tomb. The sorrow felt by His disciples (as well as the

---

[37] *Doctrine and Covenants* 58:42-43; Isaiah 1:18; 2 Nephi 31:13; Hebrews 10:17.
[38] *Bible Dictionary:* Repentance; see Dale G. Renlund, "Repentance: A Joyful Choice," *Ensign*, Nov. 2016, 121-124.
[39] Mosiah 3:19; *Doctrine and Covenants* 58:42-43; Acts 2:38; 1 Nephi 10:18-21; Jeremiah 35:15.
[40] Jeffrey R. Holland, "The Laborers in the Vineyard," *Ensign*, May 2012, 31-33.
[41] Jörg Klebingat, "Approaching the Throne of God with Confidence," *Ensign*, Nov. 2014, 34-37.
[42] Ether 12:27; Jacob 4:7; 3 Nephi 9:13-15; 2 Peter 3:9.

hosts of heaven) was immense—even the earth itself trembled.[43] However, three days later an unparalleled miracle occurred. As the crowning gift of His atoning sacrifice, Christ was resurrected.[44] The tomb is empty![45] He lives!!!

There is life after death! Our spirits can live independent of our bodies, but our bodies cannot live without our spirits.[46] When we die, our spirit separates from our bodies.[47] Our body stays on Earth, and our spirit dwells in the spirit realm—often known as the spirit world. Our personality does not change, nor the desires we had in mortality.[48] Our time in the spirit world is an era of preparation until the hour in which our spirits and bodies will be reunited (resurrected).[49] Our bodies will then be immortal.[50] No sickness, no physical pain, and no death.

After He died, Christ's spirit went to the spirit world before His resurrection. While He was there, Christ organized His "forces and appointed messengers…[to] proclaim liberty to the captives who were bound, even unto all who would repent of their sins and receive the gospel. Thus was the gospel preached to those who had died in their sins, without a knowledge of the truth, or in transgression, having rejected the prophets."[51]

God's mercy is so deep! Again, He gives those who did not have the opportunity to receive His gospel while in mortality a chance to take the steps to return home after this life. The Lord gives us every chance to have joy, but we have to do our part. Procrastination of following the Savior's path is not good; God will not be mocked.[52]

---

[43] Matthew 27:58-60; 3 Nephi 10:9; 3 Nephi 11:1-12; Matthew 27:50-51; John 20:11.
[44] Luke 24:39; *Topical Guide to the Scriptures*: Atonement; Matthew 28:1-8; 3 Nephi 11:1-17.
[45] Matthew 28:6; John 20:1-9; *Doctrine and Covenants* 76:19-24.
[46] *Bible Dictionary*: Spirit; see James 2:26; Luke 23:46.
[47] Luke 23:46; Alma 40:12-14; Luke 16:19-31.
[48] Alma 34:34.
[49] 1 Corinthians 15:22; Alma 22:14.
[50] Alma 11:43.
[51] *Doctrine and Covenants* 138:20, 30–32; 1 Corinthians 15:29; 1 Peter 3:18-20; Moses 7:37-39.
[52] Jeremiah 29:13; Galatians 6:7; Alma 34:33-34; Joshua 24:15; Psalm 119:60; 2 Nephi 28:7-12.

In result of the Lord "[breaking] the bands of death," we shall all be resurrected someday.[53] This is a free gift from Christ to all—both wicked and righteous. [54] However, where we will *dwell* after our resurrection is a result of whether we chose to take the steps to return home and diligently "practice" Christ's teachings or not.[55] In our resurrected state, we will stand before the bar of God to be judged according to our works, thoughts, words, and desires of our hearts.[56] Judgement day is not so much about what we did in our lives; rather, it is about the amount of transformation we had through the Savior's Atonement.[57] Who did we become through the steps of Christ's Atonement?[58] Did we love, learn, and grow? Did we trust God and follow His prophets?

One of the most motivating teachings about the resurrection is given by the prophet Moroni: "[During judgement day] he that is filthy shall be filthy still; and he that is righteous shall be righteous still; he that is happy shall be happy still; and he that is unhappy shall be unhappy still."[59] Do we want to live with God in a state of never-ending happiness?! The happiness starts here and now![60]

Moroni continued his teachings, "Wherefore, I would speak unto...the peaceable followers of Christ, [who] have obtained a sufficient hope by which ye can enter into the rest of the Lord, *from this time henceforth* until ye shall rest with him in heaven."[61] We can enter into His rest now! That is the miracle of Christ's joy.

In relation to our choices now and in the afterlife, it is important to Remember that you and I live in the last days before the Second Coming of the Savior. Yep, we live in what the scriptures foretold as

---

[53] Mosiah 15:8.

[54] 1 Corinthians 15:22.

[55] 1 Corinthians 15:40-42; *Doctrine and Covenants* 76:89-98; 1 Nephi 15:33-34.

[56] Mosiah 3:40; *Doctrine and Covenants* 137:9; Revelation 20:12; Alma 11:41-43; 3 Nephi 27:14-16.

[57] *Doctrine and Covenants* 76:69; Matthew 5:48; 3 Nephi 27:27.

[58] Dallin H. Oaks, "The Challenge to Become," *Ensign*, Nov. 2000, *lds.org*, The Church of Jesus Christ of Latter-day Saints, Nov. 2000 (accessed May 8, 2016).

[59] Mormon 9:14.

[60] Helaman 14:29-31; Alma 41:10.

[61] Moroni 7:3; emphasis added.

"perilous times" when "men's hearts shall fail them."[62] If anything, the calamities of the present time reveal that there is a God. Heavenly Father is indeed fulfilling His prophecies.[63] We can either constantly look at the black dot, allowing for these calamities to rule our lives, or we can hold our heads high with realization that these misfortunes are just the Lord fulfilling all His promises!

Elder Gary E. Stevenson taught, "Heavenly Father's generous compensation for living in perilous times is that we also live in the fulness of times."[64] What is being connected here is that we have the restored gospel of Christ along with technology, blessings, and opportunities that have not existed at any other time of the world!

Remember that "wickedness never was happiness."[65] When we disobey God, we are living "contrary to the nature of happiness."[66] As we strive to live in accordance with God's commandments and continually "practice" His ways, we will be enabled to more fully live with gratitude and joy in this life and in the life to come.[67]

Five Unchanging Truths

Focusing on truth gives us strength and power during our quest to experience joy and gratitude in our lives.

An increasingly well-known therapist, Jodi Hildebrandt, teaches through podcasts on the internet called *ConneXions Classroom*. Jodi teaches often about "unchanging truths." These truths are about *you*. Read them slowly and out loud if possible. Pay attention to how you feel. These are the unchanging truths about who *you* really are:

---

[62] 2 Timothy 3:1; *Doctrine and Covenants* 88:91.
[63] Isaiah 5:26; Joel 2; Matthew 24 (see *Joseph Smith-Matthew*); 2 Timothy 3-4; *Doctrine and Covenants* 45.
[64] Gary E. Stevenson, "Plain and Precious Truths," *Ensign*, Nov. 2013, 91-92.
[65] Alma 41:3.
[66] Alma 41:11.
[67] Alma 34:32-34; Alma 41:11; Colossians 3:14.

Five Unchanging Truths

1. I am <u>loved</u> (I am worthy of love).
2. I am <u>capable</u> of hard and amazing things.
3. I am <u>valuable</u>, and <u>my needs matter</u>.
4. <u>I can change</u>.
5. <u>I am enough today</u>.[68]

Due to our divine nature and heavenly heritage, these five sacred truths are never going to change! No matter your gender, height, age, body type, career, current situation, past choices…these five truths are the TRUTH about who you really are.

Satan wants you to doubt and forget your divine heritage. He is your strongest opposing force to feeling Christ's joy.[69] Subsequently, Jodi also teaches about something called distortions. She explains how "shame" (Satan) tells us that we are the opposite of the five unchanging truths. Satan's distortions most often include:

Five Most Common Distortions/Lies

1. I am <u>not</u> loved (I am not worthy of love).
2. I am <u>not</u> capable of hard or amazing things.
3. I am <u>not</u> valuable, and my needs <u>don't</u> matter.
4. I <u>cannot</u> change.
5. I am <u>not</u> enough. <u>And I never will be</u>.[70]

Those are LIES! Any negative voice or thought that alludes to the idea that you are not loveable, capable, valuable, able to change, or that you are not enough, is a distortion. You can disregard these voices and thoughts as lies from the adversary. They are some of Satan's best weapons of war. Remember, we have power to choose.

---

[68] Jodi Hildebrandt, Episode 87: "The Necessity of Distortion," Oct. 2016, *connexionsclassroom.com* (accessed Nov. 17, 2016).
[69] Moses 1:13; Moses 4:4; 2 Nephi 2:18&27; Revelation 12:7-9.
[70] Jodi Hildebrandt, Episode 106: Forum #1—"Truth vs. Distortion," April 2017, *connexionsclassroom.com* (accessed Aug. 8, 2017).

If we *choose* to repeatedly believe these lies (even just one of them), we are choosing to believe Satan over Heavenly Father. This affects our actions and will not allow us to remain on the pathway of joy.

Honestly think about how different our lives would be if we not only knew but believed those five unchanging truths about who we really are? If a distortion enters your mind, choose to fight it with an unchanging truth. We can come to know these five unchanging truths and we can work hard to fight Satan with them. More often than not, this battle takes place within us (in our little minds). This is what I like to call the "warfare of thoughts."[71]

My brother-in-law, Drew, once told me, "It has been helpful for me to learn how important it is to recognize truth and discern distortion. When people choose to believe a lie whispered by Satan, it gives the adversary power in their lives."

In the armor of God, we keep our heads/minds protected with the "helmet of salvation."[72] Our need to repeatedly review the Plan of Salvation is truly important. It helps us recognize truth and regain eternal perspective. The Plan of Salvation (Chapter 2) was one of the essential things that President Nelson taught us to focus on if we want to feel joy. Remembering the purpose of this life is essential.

As noted by Ashton before, thoughts lead to emotions, our emotions affect our actions, and "the choices we make determine our destiny."[73] We need to fight to be the "pilot at the wheel" inside our minds. The more consistently we battle Satan's lies and distorted thoughts by replacing them with truths, we begin to not only *know* but *believe* these five unchanging truths. This changes everything.

✹ ✹ ✹ ✹ ✹

These five truths can also be key in making our Sacred Time Star that much more meaningful. If we are Remembering and reviewing

---

[71] 1 Chronicles 28:9; Proverbs 23:7; 2 Corinthians 10:5; Philippians 4:8; 2 Nephi 9:39.
[72] Ephesians 6:17; 1 Thessalonians 5:8.
[73] Thomas S. Monson, "Choices," *Ensign*, May 2016, 86.

these truths while we are going for a nice walk, drawing a picture, playing the piano, going to church, etc., we will feel an enhanced protection against Satan as we begin to know, review, and believe truth. We can post these truths on our wall or in our car or on our phones. We can review them, love them, and believe them!

When I feel bombarded by Satan's lies, I feel instant relief when I begin to state truth in my mind or out loud. I know that we truly are loved, capable, valuable, able to change, and that we are enough.

To end this chapter, I would like to share some powerful real life examples of living the Smile Star.

Examples of the Smile Star

Example 1

When I was working in Provo, Utah, my friend invited me to go to a Leadership Expo. The key-note speaker was Elizabeth Smart. As she got up to speak, I noted that she had a bright countenance.

Elizabeth relayed that at age fourteen she was kidnapped at knife-point and was repeatedly raped and brain-washed for nine months until she was found. The experiences that she shared could have been in a horror film. She noted how blessed she was to have been rescued.

After her return home, several months had passed and she was really struggling. One day, Elizabeth's mom exhorted her, "The best punishment you could inflict upon your captor is to be happy. He doesn't deserve another second of your life. You can decide to be happy again and choose to move forward."

Elizabeth took her mom's advice to heart. She is now involved in promoting child abuse/abduction prevention laws and programs throughout the nation, and she wrote an inspiring book about her experiences called *My Story*. Though what Elizabeth went through was horrific, she has chosen to make what was a "black dot" a part of the "white" in her life as she blesses others with similar trials. In the end it was her choice, and she chose the path of progression.

Her mom's insights can help us in the process of forgiving others and ourselves. Her insights are also relatable to our daily struggles against Satan. The devil and his servants constantly battle us and they try daily to be our captors. The best retribution is not to sulk in our misdeeds of the past, nor should we become absorbed with the black dots in our lives. We must move forward with "steadfastness in Christ."[74] That is the ultimate punishment to the ultimate captor. The Ultimate Rescuer is on our side, even the Savior of the world. Satan does not deserve another second of our lives. Satan is the prince of misery, and Christ is the Author of Joy.[75] *Be grateful and smile. Christ is joy.*

<u>Example 2</u>

My ancestor, Lydia Knight, was a woman of impeccable faith. She was married to Newel Knight, who was a stalwart man and one of Joseph Smith's truest friends. Remember the pioneer stories in the previous chapter? Newel and Lydia took part in those severe challenges. She waded through continual trials throughout her life, but her motto was: "God Rules." She was not saying it in the way teenagers in the 90's would say, "That totally rules man!" No, she was saying it with the utmost respect that God rules all, and He is in charge. I have felt strongly that I should share a part of her story with you; her life was a legacy of the Smile Star.

We will begin with her family being harassed by mobs from Jackson to Clay County, Missouri:

> Through this time of trouble she remained calm—
> perhaps because enough grief had already touched her life
> and she knew how to fit joy into the corners. When a sister

---

[74] 2 Nephi 31:20.
[75] Hebrews 5:9; 2 Samuel 22:2.

complained about their trials, she said, "Be calm; let your heart rather be filled with humblest prayer, that God will turn aside their wicked purposes." She managed not to hate the mob…her faith was undiminished.

During the trek west, her greatest trial came. Well out into Indian country her beloved husband Newel Knight became ill.

At first Lydia prayed for him to be spared, but as his pain grew worse, she prayed for the Lord to release him. He died. But to sustain her she had [received] the promise [from] the Prophet: "Sister Lydia, great are your blessings. The Lord loves you, and will overrule all your sorrows and afflictions."[76]

The evening Newel was buried. No lumber could be had, so Lydia had one of her wagon-boxes made into a rude coffin. The day was excessively cold, and some of the brethren had their fingers and feet frozen while digging the grave and performing the last offices of love for their honored captain and brother. As [Lydia] looked out upon the wilderness of snow and saw the men bearing away all that was left of her husband, it seemed that the flavor of life had fled and left only dregs, bitter, unavailing sorrow. But as she grew calmer she whispered, "God rules!" [77]

[Alone in Indian country with seven children and pregnant with her eighth, Lydia pressed on].

At some point, Lydia, burdened by having to continue on without Newel wondered out loud in her cabin why he had left her. Then [as she spoke] Newel appeared to her and stood by her side, with a lovely smile on his face, and said: "Be calm, let not sorrow overcome you. It was necessary that I should go. I was needed behind the veil to represent the true condition of this camp and people. You

[76] Jan J. Williams and LaRea G. Strebel, " Lydia Knight: 'God Rules' Was Her Motto," Aug. 1977, *lds.org* (accessed June 20, 2016).
[77] "Lydia Knight," *geni.com*, 2008 (accessed June 19, 2016).

cannot fully comprehend it now; but the time will come when you shall know why I left you and our little ones. Therefore, dry up your tears. Be patient, I will go before you and protect you in your journeying. And you and your little ones shall never perish for lack of food."[78]

So Lydia continued to live and serve as she always had. Her children shivered through the winter in a hut built in front of a hillside cave. She spent one cold night with rain coming through a half-finished roof on her and her newborn child. Even after better lodgings had been found, Lydia had to work, raising crops and washing and sewing, in order to survive and raise money to join the trek west. She had not forgotten her obedience to the Lord. After her husband died she still had a yoke of oxen and a wagon, yet because she and her infant could not make the trip at that time, she consecrated the wagon and animals for another family to use. When Lydia did leave, she and her children walked most of the way...finally joining the saints in Salt Lake Valley.

Even after she joined the Saints in Utah, Lydia's trials were not over: after a few unhappy years of a third marriage, she was back to teaching school to support her children. Later she accepted a proposal from a widower named McClellan, and married for the fourth time. Twenty years of a good relationship followed, and then she was left a widow again at the age of sixty-eight. She served as a temple worker in the St. George Temple almost until her death in April 1884. There in the temple, where eternity seems only a footstep away, she looked forward to returning to live with Newel, the man to whom she had been given for eternity.

Four times in her life Lydia Knight was left alone with children to support, but she proved herself worthy of the

---

[78] William G. Hartley, *Stand By My Servant Joseph*, 2003, 425-426.

Lord's trust. She never lost the great courage she showed during the Missouri persecutions when Newel was called from her side to guard the brethren. "My dear, be careful of our little ones tonight," he said. "I must go out and join my brethren who are on guard. You won't be afraid, will you?" Lydia answered, "Newel, God rules."[79]

Lydia is a legacy of moving forward with faith while allowing her afflictions to be "swallowed up in the joy of Christ."[80] Through her deep trials, her life's motto kept her on the path of joy. God Rules. *Be grateful and smile. Christ is joy.*

Example 3

While working in the hospital, I sat down to chat with an elderly patient about his life. He relayed to me that he had grown up during the Great Depression. I asked him about those circumstances. With his feeble voice he responded, "Well, I will tell you something. I know what it is like to be homeless and poor. Everything we enjoyed came with much hard work and effort. In order to eat, we had to hunt and trap. If we wanted different clothes, we sewed them ourselves." I listened intently.

He continued, "Living conditions were extremely cramped. With my parents and seven siblings, we lived in something similar to a tent for almost four years. For our 'family vacations' we would go hiking for a few days."

I was humbled by his experiences, and I asked him, "My friend, with all those severe challenges, were you happy?"

Without hesitation, he responded, "Kayla, we were poorer than dirt, but we didn't know it. We focused on the basics. I may have been happier during the Great Depression than I was when I had all

---

[79] Jan J. Williams and LaRea G. Strebel, "Lydia Knight: 'God Rules' Was Her Motto," Aug. 1977, *lds.org* (accessed June 20, 2016).
[80] Alma 31:38.

the necessities of life and more. I have learned that perspective is the key to happy days."

I was so touched by this man. I saw him pass through many hard days, but he could be seen joking and laughing amidst the struggle. *Be grateful and smile. Christ is joy.*

Example 4

A powerful example of living the spirit and attitude of the Smile Star was the prophet, President Gordon B. Hinckley.

Some of his famous phrases include: "be believing," "be happy," "don't get discouraged," "be clean," "things will work out!" [81] President Hinckley taught:

> [In the ride of life], the trick is to thank the Lord for letting you have the ride; and really, isn't it a wonderful ride? Enjoy it! Laugh about it! Sing about it! Remember the words of the writer of Proverbs:
>
> "A merry heart doeth good like a medicine: but a broken spirit drieth the bones" (Proverbs 17:22).
>
> Let there be something of a light tone in your life. Let there be fun and happiness, a sense of humor...laugh occasionally at things that are funny. Life is to be enjoyed, not just endured.[82]

His teachings have helped me through tough times. When I remember that life is to be enjoyed, hard situations seem to be less daunting and the sun seems to shine a little brighter through the clouds. President Hinckley also encouraged:

> Don't be gloomy. Do not dwell on unkind things. Stop seeking out the storms and enjoy more fully the sunlight. Even if you are not happy, put a smile on your face.

---

[81] Jeffrey R. Holland, "President Gordon B. Hinckley: Stalwart and Brave He Stands," *Ensign*, June 1995, 4.
[82] Gordon B. Hinckley, "Stand True and Faithful," *Ensign*, May 1996, 93-94.

'Accentuate the positive.' Look a little deeper for the good. Go forward in life with a twinkle in your eye and a smile on your face, with great and strong purpose in your heart. Love life.[83]

I know that we can indeed accentuate the positive in our own lives and in the lives of others. This perspective and desire helps us see more as the Savior sees and live as He lived.

Be grateful and smile. Christ is joy.

Example 5

Another great example of the Smile Star was the apostle Joseph B. Wirthlin. He taught of a powerful teaching he received from his mom that guided him through the challenges of life. This powerful perspective can help us in our journeys of life as well:

> When I was young I loved playing sports, and I have many fond memories of those days. But not all of them are pleasant. I remember one day after my football team lost a tough game, I came home feeling discouraged. My mother was there [and] she listened to my sad story…the advice my mother gave to me…has stayed with me all my life.
>
> "Joseph," she said, "come what may, and love it."
>
> I think she may have meant that every life has peaks and shadows and times when it seems that the birds don't sing and bells don't ring. Yet in spite of discouragement and adversity, those who are happiest seem to have a way of learning from difficult times, becoming stronger, wiser, and happier as a result. How can we love days that are filled with sorrow? We can't—at least not in the moment. I don't think my mother was suggesting that we suppress discouragement or deny the reality of pain. I don't think she was suggesting that we smother unpleasant truths beneath a cloak of pretended happiness. But I do believe

---

[83] Gordon B. Hinckley, "Words of the Prophet: The Spirit of Optimism," *New Era*, July 2001, 4-6.

that the way we react to adversity can be a major factor in how happy and successful we can be in life.

If we approach adversities wisely, our hardest times can be times of greatest growth, which in turn can lead toward times of greatest happiness.[84]

Elder Wirthlin taught four things that can assist us in our mortal journey as we press forward during hard times. These four crucial teachings he emphasized were:

1. Learn to *laugh*.
2. Seek for the *eternal perspective*.
3. Understand that *God compensates* the faithful for every loss.
4. *Trust* in the Lord.[85]

I am deeply grateful for Elder Wirthlin's teachings and example. I have learned through experience that what he taught is true. Come what may, and love it. *Be grateful and smile. Christ is joy.*

✹ ✹ ✹ ✹ ✹

Smiling truly is a declaration of the heart. At times when we may not feel happy, we can still feel an underlying joy. Christ is the only true source of joy. This Star truly brightens all the other Stars.

Though we may have a lot of "black dots" in our lives, we can fill our views with the "white" around us. We can be grateful and smile because in Jesus Christ we find true joy. President Dieter F. Uchtdorf taught:

> Everyone's situation is different, and the details of each life are unique. Nevertheless, I have learned that there is something that would take away the bitterness that may come into our lives. There is one thing we can do to make life sweeter, more joyful, even glorious. We can be grateful!
> ...Could I suggest that we see gratitude as a disposition, a

---

[84] Joseph B. Wirthlin, "Come What May, and Love It," *Ensign*, Nov. 2008, 26-28; see 2 Nephi 2:25.
[85] Joseph B. Wirthlin, "Come What May, and Love It," *Ensign*, Nov. 2008, 26-28.

way of life that stands independent of our current situation? In other words, I'm suggesting that instead of being thankful for things, we focus on being thankful in our circumstances—whatever they may be.

When we are grateful to God in our circumstances, we can experience gentle peace in the midst of tribulation. In grief, we can still lift up our hearts in praise. In pain, we can glory in Christ's Atonement. In the cold of bitter sorrow, we can experience the closeness and warmth of heaven's embrace.[86]

The 5 Star Day will not feel as fulfilling whenever we are missing any of the Stars—that includes the Smile Star. Christ's joy permeates our souls as we let Him into our lives through gratitude. God wants us to experience joy; may we show Him our gratitude and desire to obtain a fullness of joy by enduring the challenges we face in this life with faith and hope.

All the Stars in the 5 Star Day working together can allow for our spiritual health to thrive. This leads us to our next chapter which talks about the 5 Star Day's role in emotional, physical, and mental health. There are supporting actions that can allow for healing and divine help through emotional storms.

[86] Dieter F. Uchtdorf, "Grateful in Any Circumstances," May 2014, *Ensign*, 70, 75-77.

Chapter 9

Supplemental Stars

I WOULD LIKE TO take a moment to address any who have struggled with emotional and mental turmoil. I think we all have to some degree, and I acknowledge that many cases can be severe.

Throughout my life, I have occasionally been affected by mental and emotional distress. In those states, the best way I can describe it is that I feel numb. It can feel confusing and hard to recognize the feelings of the Spirit. The Word of Wisdom (God's law of health), and the 5 Star Day get me through.[1] These give me hope that the light will come, and there will be better days once again.

During those times, it is of great importance to pay attention to our thoughts. We usually find distortions and lies of Satan taking over. We must fight those negative voices with truths!

In addition, there are certain actions that are extremely helpful during those emotional storms. These actions are what my dear friend likes to call **Supplemental Stars**:

* ✱ Speak Truth
* ✱ Sleep
* ✱ Sweat (Exercise/Drink Water/Eat Well)
* ✱ Shower
* ✱ Support
* ✱ Slow Down
* ✱ Shine/Sunshine

---

[1] *Doctrine and Covenants* 89.

At this time, I would like to share some insights from this friend of mine. She openly shares perspective into her experience with implementing the 5 Star Day amidst depression. In combination with the Supplemental Stars, she relates how peace, healing, and happiness flowed into her life again. In her own words, she relays:

In this chapter, I share my own personal experience with clinical depression. I do not share these things lightly. In time, I have come to realize the critical and undeniable importance of consistently implementing these Supplemental Stars in my life. It has been invaluable to me, especially in my down times, to have these Stars as a clear, simple formula of concrete action items and tools that I can focus on and channel my energy toward. I have found that doing these simple things tangibly helps me have the strength to combat the darkness and push away the fog of depression. The Supplemental Stars have been absolutely essential in my healing process and to this day I implement them regularly.

My experiences of being engulfed in the overwhelming fog of depression helped me to truly learn the critical importance of prioritizing my day in perspective of the basics.

During a more stable emotional phase, the consistent results of living the 5 Star Day in my life was tremendous in that it transformed a "not so good" day into a genuinely "good" day, and it could turn a "good" day into a "great/spectacular" day.

On the contrary, when I felt submerged and tossed in the depths of depression's waves, the 5 Star Day was my lifeline. In those survival modes, I experienced that choosing to implement the simple and vital choices of these 5 primary stars each day was like choosing to grab hold of flotation devices. The 5 Star Day did not take away the wave(s) or the fact that I continued to be submerged or tossed about, but these simple choices helped my head stay above water for sustaining breath time and time again.

I typed it up, printed it out, and hung the 5 Star Day on my wall. I would look at it often as a reminder to focus on the basics. I didn't view it as a checklist, it was my lifeline.

The Scripture Study, Sincere Prayer, and Service Stars were particularly my personal lifelines. I will be honest, I had a harder time engaging in the Sacred

Time and Smile Stars. To me, back then, the Sacred Time Star meant "Self-Reflection" and the Smile Star meant that I needed to be showing my pearly whites freely throughout the day. This presented some challenges for me.

Self-reflecting for the Sacred Time Star was difficult to do because Satan's lies pointed me to reflect on what I had NOT done, or all of the mistakes I had made that day. I usually walked away feeling that I was not enough, which is the furthest thing from the outcome of living the Sacred Time Star. Self-reflection is still super important, but I was going about it the wrong way. It was so helpful when Kayla reached the point in her studies to focus the Sacred Time Star more on Remembering and seeking to have an honest connection with heaven each day—time where I was inclined to look up instead of down.

Smiling was definitely a challenge in those heavy waves of thick darkness and fog. I felt so exhausted, so overwhelmed; I felt bombarded emotionally, mentally, and spiritually. I was in survival mode much of the time. Smiling was the last thing I wanted to do. I had to make a conscious choice to smile. I had to force it. To help me in my efforts there were days that I chose to "practice" smiling. I would do this as I drove in my car. It felt really awkward and forced. Sometimes the people I was next to at the stoplights would look over at me and I would just feel so silly, but I did it anyway. There were times I'd end up chuckling for a moment at my cheesy self along the way. It did tend to give me a little needed boost in propelling me toward the surface of the wave by merely going through the motions of what I thought embodied this Smile Star. I later learned and incorporated the true meaning of the Smile Star, which embodies more of seeking to have an attitude of gratitude and joy. That was powerful to me to make that shift. Living in gratitude and joy can help bring a tangible smile.

I do have to say that my capacity for putting into action the 5 Stars seemed to look and feel different during waves of depression versus times of less emotional/mental turmoil. I came to know that God knows perfectly just how difficult it is amidst the crashing waves of depression to muster up the faith, channel the energy, and put forth the effort to do these vital things. I learned that even though I didn't usually feel like doing the 5 Star Day (or much of anything for that matter when engulfed in depression) that if I simply tried, or as Al Carroway calls it "real try," that I was blessed.[2] The Lord recognizes and

---

[2] Al Fox Carroway, *More Than the Tattooed Mormon*, Nov. 2015.

readily honors our efforts, our "real tries," to follow Him and to live the 5 Star Day regardless of what that looks like or feels like in comparison to anything or anyone else.

My efforts to live the 5 Star Day would resurface me and sustain me. With my head "above water" I would have moments, hours, and sometimes days (very few and far between), where I felt like "myself" again and I took those experiences as miracles and blessings. I deeply yearned to overcome, to heal, to make it to shore, and to find respite from these waves.

Over time I found that there were some specific things that I could do once my head was above water that consistently served as sustaining "breaths and strokes" that actually helped me move forward and progress toward healing. These things are what I call the Supplemental Stars to the 5 Star Day. I am very passionate about these Stars and have personally found that they truly support our physical/emotional/overall wellbeing. These things are interrelated to the irreplaceable 5 Stars, and yet come with their own power. They are:

- ✱ *Speak Truth*
- ✱ *Sweat (Exercise/Drink Water/Eat Well)*
- ✱ *Shower*
- ✱ *Sleep*
- ✱ *Support*
- ✱ *Slow Down*
- ✱ *Shine/Sunshine*

These Stars, like the 5 Star Day, are simple and yet have such a profound impact for good. I will talk briefly about the wisdom and strength found in each of these Supplemental Stars that I have discovered through my own experiences with living them.

Speak Truth—

I cannot emphasize the absolute importance of thinking, speaking, reviewing, and believing the Five Unchanging Truths about who we really are.[3] I learned the vital importance of staying connected with my feelings and recognizing when I

---

[3] Jodi Hildebrandt, Episode 41: "Self-Care & Responsibility (Part 2)," Feb. 2015, *connexionsclassroom.com* (accessed March 26, 2017).

was feeling shame, despair, profound sadness, gloom, and anxiety. I was suppressing a lot of the uncomfortable emotions I was having. These severe emotions came as a result of the shame messages that I was believing. I would shun or not allow myself to feel my negative feelings because admitting I was experiencing such emotions often caused more shame because I did not feel like it was ok to be feeling that way. I learned that the uncomfortable emotions I was feeling needed to be recognized and allowed to be felt, as sometimes difficult as that was.

I have learned that no emotion is inherently good or bad. Emotions are neutral. Our emotions are there to send us important messages. They invite us to take a look at what is going on in our lives and examine if something is needing our attention or if something is amiss and needing an adjustment or course correction. Choosing to stay connected with my emotions by checking in regularly with how I am feeling has been absolutely crucial in overcoming my war with depression.

I have learned that once I allow myself to feel whatever uncomfortable emotions I am feeling, and have validated that it is ok for me to feel what I am feeling. I am then ready to process these emotions and work to let them go. At this point, I take a look at the thoughts that these emotions are linked to and discern if they are actually grounded in Truth.

On my journey to healing I have come to find that believing lies or half-truths about myself, about others, or about my situation (going into distortion) has been closely linked to my feelings of self-hatred and despair. Through being more connected with my emotions and then tracing them back to my thoughts to see what was driving those emotions, I have been able to identify the lies/shame messages, kick them out, replace them with the Truth, and then experience what to me feels like a miracle. The negative and uncomfortable feelings driven by the shame and lies go away faster and stay away longer than anything else I have tried. This is profound. It has absolutely been life changing for me to recognize the distortions in my thoughts, let them go, feel the emotional distress follow, and return to living in Truth.[4] It has been so freeing and healing.

---

[4] Jodi Hildebrandt, Episode 70: "Truth Declarations," May 2016, *connexionsclassroom.com* (accessed July 20, 2016).

Make It a 5 Star Day!

Again, I invite you to read the section where Kayla reiterates Jodi's teachings about the Five Unchanging Truths (Chapter 8: Smile Star) for a refresher if you feel the need. Living in Truth results in more happiness, peace, freedom, perspective, empathy, joy, charity, honesty, and connection to God, self, and others. I do not know if I can adequately stress the importance of staying in Truth and the profound blessings of doing so. This is something you do not have to take my word for, give it a try. It is so worth it!

Sleep—

Sleep, glorious sleep!!! If there is one tangible effort that I have control over that seems to affect my ability to function in more of a "thrive" zone than just in a "survive" zone, it is getting the proper amount (meaning not too much or too little) of rest/sleep. I have found it extremely difficult to develop good sleep hygiene amidst years of pushing myself mentally with intense academic course loads, physically through very competitive sports, emotionally through multiple pregnancies within a short period of time with little support, and also chronically overextending myself. I was pushing myself to the limit of what I could handle, spreading myself very thin, running faster than I had strength, and then not adequately resting, relaxing, and allowing a pace that permitted self-care. Sleep seemed to chronically be the afterthought and not the priority. I have known for a long time that something needed to change.

In the healing process of my depression I have concentrated my efforts on going to bed earlier and rising earlier. It has been one of the hardest things I have ever done. It feels like quite a fight to force myself to do this. However, it has made such a profound difference in my life whenever I do.

I have found that my body actually communicates to me when it is tired (I had ignored these cues for so many years). Through my experiences of listening to my body's cues, I have found that my body personally operates best with 8-9 hours of sleep, which is much more than what my husband can operate on. I have learned that I need to take personal responsibility for taking care of my body. No one else can sleep for me. No one else can feel those signals from my body that communicate my need for rest. This seems so basic. Simplifying, slowing down, and returning to the basics in a lot of aspects of my life have helped me to gain strength and to heal.

I do feel to mention that most often in my bouts with depression it did not matter how long I stayed in bed or how much sleep I got, getting out of bed felt like an insurmountable task. There are no words adequate to describe how this feels.

Looking back, I realize that it wasn't the tired, fatigued, and sluggish feelings alone that made it so hard to get out of bed. There were days that I stayed in bed for amounts of time far beyond the hours of sleep my body needed. I would lay there awake for sometimes hours feeling unable to get out of bed due to the intense feelings of doom and gloom, the dread and overwhelming weight of any responsibilities and expectations hanging over me, and complete lack of desire to do anything. On these days I also felt a deep discouragement and self-loathing, which feelings were rooted in shame, because I was still in bed and I felt as though the day was already a lost cause. "Why bother getting up now? I already failed" were some of the thoughts I would think.

What I have learned, especially in these intense bouts, is that if I could do my very best to stick to the amount of sleep that I came to know that my body needs, that the dark clouds would consistently disperse to a degree and a measure of energy would eventually come after I made the choice to get my feet on the ground and be up and about. I have learned to tell myself that the intense feelings that I am feeling laying there are real and that it is okay to feel them, AND that they will not last forever. And also that if I will trust myself to get up when I have had the proper amount of sleep that things will improve.

On days when I slept in and did not choose to get up, I have found it extremely important to be kind to and patient with myself. I must seek to remember the truth in that no day is a lost cause, no matter how late I slept in, and that despite my choice to sleep in that I am still enough and the eternal and unchanging truths still do and will ever still uphold.

Do you know how much sleep your body functions best on? I encourage you to find out. Proper sleep hygiene is a very powerful and healing tool that we generally have control over. When I take responsibility to care for and honor my needs and give my body adequate sleep, as hard as it is, I find that I consistently function better. It is worth it.

Make It a 5 Star Day!

S w eat—

Working out is something that creates endorphins in our bodies that help improve mood. I have found that particularly cardio workouts help pierce through the fog of depression or help blow away gray clouds that are starting to close in. If it is possible, getting in a 30 minute cardio workout 3-5 times a week will greatly help muster strength and make strides toward the shore in the waves of depression.

The "w" and the "eat" that are separately underlined in the "sweat" stand for drinking enough Water to avoid dehydration and Eating a nutritious diet, rich in vegetables, fruits, and whole grains. Overeating and undereating can mask the emotions for a time, but does not solve anything. I cannot emphasize the importance of taking care of our physical health to positively impact our emotional health. They are interrelated. They are both of equal importance.

Shower—

I have found that making time for a shower each day and then getting dressed and ready for the day has been incredibly helpful and healing. Amidst depression I did not feel the desire to get up, let alone get in the shower and get read for the day. Regardless, when I would make this a priority I found that it helped every time! In my shower time I would envision the gloom just washing off me and going down the drain. I would try to clear my mind and relax my body. During this time I would try to really remember and re-center on the most important things—as emphasized with the Sacred Time Star.

After my shower I found that when I chose to put on my make-up and get dressed in clothes that were not workout clothes or pj's that I felt an increase in energy, confidence, and ability to function, which made a very big difference as well.

Support—

Having a support group of a few key friends and family members that I could turn to in my very low times has also been crucial. I needed people who would listen, validate, empathize, and be willing to just pray for me. The healing influence that my husband's support, patience, and unconditional love have had on me on my road to overcoming my depression has been incredibly profound. There are no words for my gratitude.

I had stretches where despite my efforts I would not know how to continue on. In these times I would turn to the Lord by asking for a priesthood blessing to be blessed with the support, strength, reassurance, and guidance I so deeply needed. These priesthood blessings have been absolutely priceless to me. It is one way that I have felt undeniably connected to heaven and can feel of His matchless love and awareness of me and even the very details of my life.

Another one of the crucial steps I took toward healing was my choice to go to therapy. I feel strongly that this choice to seek professional support through therapy was inspired and guided by the Lord. My therapist has been one of those dear friends in whom I have been able to trust and turn to for the support and tools that I have needed. I have learned that we must regard our emotional health on the same level as our physical health. If someone had a broken leg, we would not tell them to just walk it off. We would not look down on them for seeking the medical attention their broken leg needs. Emotional health should be no different. It affects our ability to function and thrive just as our physical health does.

Elder Jeffrey R. Holland counseled us:

> *If things continue to be debilitating, seek the advice of reputable people with certified training, professional skills, and good values. Be honest with them about your history and your struggles. Prayerfully and responsibly consider the counsel they give and the solutions they prescribe. If you had appendicitis, God would expect you to seek a priesthood blessing and get the best medical care available. So too with emotional disorders. Our Father in Heaven expects us to use all of the marvelous gifts He has provided in this glorious dispensation.[5]*

I recognize and admit that seeking out the professional help and support that I needed emotionally took a great deal of humility and courage. In going to therapy and experiencing what it is, I have come to know that seeking emotional healing and support truly is something that we need not be ashamed of. I am so grateful that I came to recognize my profound need for help and that I was

---

[5] Jeffrey R. Holland, "Like a Broken Vessel," *Ensign*, Nov. 2013, 40-42.

195

blessed to have the courage to reach out. My therapist greatly assisted me through my depression on my road to emotional healing.

Medication can also be helpful, and necessary for some. There are many doctors and professionals who can be important members of the support team to help us work toward healing.

Slow Down—

There is a tendency in today's world to overload ourselves. The pace of life is seemingly ever increasing. I found myself personally putting pressure on myself to do in a day that which one person might have the capacity to do in a week. I know that in my times of struggle and particularly when I have been believing shame messages about myself that this is particularly the case.

I tended to overload my plate to try to mask the uncomfortable emotions and try to convince myself that I was enough. I said yes, yes, yes to things beyond my capacity and learned firsthand that there was nothing that I could do that was sufficient to convince myself of the truth (that I am actually already enough!). I may have felt a temporary reprieve at times as I looked at all of the things I had done, but those feelings were fleeting and in the end I would come up short every time. It was like trying to fill a bottomless bucket. I was running faster than I had strength.⁶ This pattern of living consistently led to burn out and break down.

Elder Holland taught, "Fatigue is the common enemy of us all—so slow down, rest up, replenish, and refill. Physicians promise us that if we do not take time to be well, we most assuredly will take time later on to be ill."⁷

I have since learned that there is profound wisdom in Slowing down, in Simplifying, in prioritizing Self-care, in Setting boundaries, and in Saying no. There is a great need to have both inner and outer boundaries firmly in place that nobly protect our commitment to the 5 Star Day and the Supplemental Stars. This is especially the case in the midst of the emotional, mental, physical, and spiritual storms of life that we will face. We must slow down and focus on the basics so that we make sure we are making the time to be well and stay well.

President Uchtdorf wisely taught us:

---

⁶ Mosiah 7:27; *Doctrine and Covenants* 10:4.
⁷ Jeffrey R. Holland, "Like a Broken Vessel," *Ensign*, Nov. 2013, 40-42.

One of the things we learn from studying the growth of trees is that during seasons when conditions are ideal, trees grow at a normal rate. However, during seasons when growing conditions are not ideal, trees slow down their growth and devote their energy to the basic elements necessary for survival...Therefore, it is good advice to slow down a little, steady the course, and focus on the essentials when experiencing adverse conditions.

This is a simple but critical lesson to learn. It may seem logical when put in terms of trees…, but it's surprising how easy it is to ignore this lesson when it comes to applying these principles in our own daily lives. When stress levels rise, when distress appears, when tragedy strikes, too often we attempt to keep up the same frantic pace or even accelerate, thinking somehow that the more rushed our pace, the better off we will be.

One of the characteristics of modern life seems to be that we are moving at an ever-increasing rate, regardless of turbulence or obstacles.

Let's be honest; it's rather easy to be busy. We all can think up a list of tasks that will overwhelm our schedules. Some might even think that their self-worth depends on the length of their to-do list. They flood the open spaces in their time with lists of meetings and minutia—even during times of stress and fatigue. Because they unnecessarily complicate their lives, they often feel increased frustration, diminished joy, and too little sense of meaning in their lives.

Strength comes not from frantic activity but from being settled on a firm foundation of truth and light. It comes from placing our attention and efforts on the basics of the restored gospel of Jesus Christ. It comes from paying attention to the divine things that matter most.

Let us simplify our lives a little. Let us make the changes necessary to refocus our lives on the sublime beauty of the simple, humble path of Christian discipleship—the path that leads always toward a life of meaning, gladness, and peace.[8]

---

[8] Dieter F. Uchtdorf, "Of Things That Matter Most," *Ensign*, Oct. 2010, 19-22.

May we ever heed this counsel and put these prophetic words to the test and see the miracles of healing, peace, and deep joy that will flow into our lives. I invite you to see for yourself.

Shine/Sunshine—

For so long I lived in a state of what felt like numbness. "Was I still in there?" I would wonder at times. I realized that I no longer participated in many of the things that I once found great joy in like organized sports, art, music, working out, socializing with friends. It wasn't only that I didn't participate in these things like I used to, I didn't even have the desire to.

It was a journey to find and remember my passions, dreams, and goals. Part of that journey was to remember that I did have them. I WAS still in there. I joined a gym and I forced myself to go, even if I only stayed for fifteen minutes at a time some days. I didn't want to go, and would sometimes sit in the parking lot for a very long time before I was able to get myself to go in, but I was always glad that I went and I was then able to be in a better position to function that day. I also decided to sign up for an art class. There is something so healing to me about getting lost in art and creating something. Deciding to engage again in these things started me on a journey of realizing the importance of making time for self-development which has made such a difference and helped me progress toward thriving and shining again.

Also, there is such a healing power in simply being in nature, taking a walk, sitting on a park bench or the beach, and just taking in God's creations. Getting out of the house and breathing in fresh air with the sun on my face has such a rejuvenating power to my soul. Opening up the blinds and letting the sunlight brighten our home makes a profound difference in the mood I feel therein. On another note, I would say that listening to uplifting music has been like sunshine to my soul in particularly hard waves/days. Lyrics that speak truths and melodies that bring peace and comfort help bring warmth to dark and foggy days. Uplifting music has been very important to me to keep me going. It doesn't take away the crashing wave but it can rejuvenate the soul, restore hope, and help foster perseverance. I try to live with a song in my heart, sunshine in my soul.

There is wisdom and strength found in these Supplemental Stars that have assisted me on my journey to healing from depression. It was also a helpful guide for my spouse to be able to know the crucial and simple things he could support me in focusing on daily.

I will say this, EVERY SINGLE ONE of the Supplemental Stars and irreplaceable 5 Star Day actions have been crucial for functioning and taking steps of healing during my darkest days and bouts with depression. I am reminded frequently of the effectiveness of implementing these simple tools as I continue to incorporate them.

I want to share some words of guidance and hope by Elder Jeffrey R. Holland that were spoken to both those who struggle with depression and their loved ones:

> *So how do you best respond when mental or emotional challenges confront you or those you love? Above all, never lose faith in your Father in Heaven, who loves you more than you can comprehend. As President Monson said to the Relief Society sisters…"That love never changes…It is there for you when you are sad or happy, discouraged or hopeful. God's love is there for you whether or not you feel you deserve [it]. It is simply always there." Never, ever doubt that, and never harden your heart. Faithfully pursue the time-tested devotional practices that bring the Spirit of the Lord into your life. Seek the counsel of those who hold keys for your spiritual well-being. Ask for and cherish priesthood blessings. Take the sacrament every week, and hold fast to the perfecting promises of the Atonement of Jesus Christ. Believe in miracles. I have seen so many of them come when every other indication would say that hope was lost. Hope is never lost. If those miracles do not come soon or fully or seemingly at all, remember the Savior's own anguished example: if the bitter cup does not pass, drink it and be strong, trusting in happier days ahead.[9]*

I know that what Elder Holland taught us is absolutely true. Looking back, I can clearly see and feel that through consistently living the 5 Star Day (i.e. faithfully pursuing the time-tested devotional practices that bring the Spirit of the Lord into my life) during bouts of depression, I have gained a powerful

[9] Jeffrey R. Holland, "Like a Broken Vessel," *Ensign*, Nov. 2013, 40-42.

understanding of the reality of our Savior Jesus Christ and a knowledge that happier days ahead are indeed possible through Him. I now know that His power and strength flows into our lives when we make Him our daily reality. It truly was His infinite Love, His perfect understanding, and His unfailing constancy in my life that saw me through every gloomy day, every fog-filled week, and carried me through my darkest hours.

I have known about Jesus Christ and that He is the Savior of the world since I was a child. In walking this road with Him by my side, I have come to know Him for myself as my personal Savior. I have become so humbly aware of my need for Him, and I am so deeply grateful for what He means to me in my life. Christ has become my most constant, and trusted, friend. I have come to know that His Atonement is not only something important we read about in the scriptures and hear about from the prophets. He atoned for us not only to cleanse us from our sins; He atoned for me, and for you, to provide us with the enabling power, and strength, that we need in our daily lives to not only survive but to become.

I experienced a life-changing transformation—inside and out—when I decided not only to know that Christ is my Savior, but to believe it. To believe Him when He said: "I will not leave you comfortless: I will come to you," "Take my yoke upon you...and you shall find rest in your souls," "I am the light of the world: he that followeth me shall not walk in darkness, but shall have the light of life." [10]

This transformation took me one step at a time out of the fog. It was not immediate, it took time. The pace was painfully slow at times. He gave me the strength to be patient. With His help I was able to loosen my grip—and with time, let go—of the lies that I was holding on to. Those distortions weighed me down heavily and held me captive to the thick fog. With His grace, mercy, and truth, I was able to pierce through the darkness and again feel the warmth and light I so craved in my life again. He is not only a way back into the light but the way. I have come to know that with Him I am enough. Today and always.

Through the consistent implementation of the 5 Star Day, and with the Supplemental Stars used according to my day-to-day needs, Christ truly has become my daily reality like never before. This has changed everything.

---

[10] John 14: 18; Matthew 11:29; John 8:12.

This book was not complete without this chapter. Working as a team, the Supplemental Stars and the 5 Star Day can give us the necessary strength and perspective in our journey here on earth. We are capable, and we are so valuable to the Lord. I greatly appreciate my friend who shared these wonderful insights and experiences with us. There is simple yet profound wisdom in the Supplemental Stars; they are inspired. Through experience, I can testify of that.

Our bodies are gifts from God, may we show Him that we cherish these gifts. You are everything the Lord tells you that you are and more. Jesus thought you were worth saving. He loves you.[11] He wants to help us in every way He can, and He has given us tools to build our lives in the way that will lead to eternal progression and eternal life. In support of what my friend taught, I too want to bear my humble witness that the 5 Star Day, and the application of the Supplemental Stars as needed, can truly change everything.

---

[11] Moses 7:28-35; 1 John 4:19; 1 Corinthians 2:9.

Chapter 10

Conclusion and Testimonies

ALRIGHT MY FRIEND, it is time to go from learning about the 5 Star Day to applying it. The 5 Star Day is meant to simplify our lives. It helps us prioritize the most important things and build our foundation on Christ.

Again, the Lord and His holy prophets teach us of these same five actions, and plead for us to put them to practice. The 5 Star Day is just an easy way to help us remember. In the year 2016 a modern-day apostle, D. Todd Christofferson, taught about different strategies for putting the Lord at the center of our lives:

> You and I can put Christ at the center of our lives and become one with Him as He is one with the Father. We could begin by stripping everything out of our lives and then putting it back together in priority order with the Savior at the center. We would first put in place the things that make it possible always to **remember** Him—**frequent prayer**, studying/pondering the **scriptures**, thoughtful study of **apostolic teachings**, weekly preparation to partake of the **sacrament worthily…recording** and **remembering** what the Spirit and experience teach us about **discipleship**. In this way the essential will not be crowded out of our lives by the merely good.[1]

---

[1] D. Todd Christofferson, "How to Make Christ the Center of Our Lives," *New Era*, Oct. 2016, 48; emphasis added; see John 17:20-23.

Over 40 years ago, President James E. Faust taught of five ways to have a personal relationship with the Savior:

> May I suggest five beginning, essential measures which will greatly clear the channel for a daily flow of "living water" from the very source of the spring, even the Redeemer Himself.
>
> First: A daily communion involving prayer. A **fervent, sincere prayer** is a two-way communication which will do much to bring His Spirit flowing like healing water to help with the hardships, aches, and pains we all face...
>
> Second: A **daily selfless service to another**...
>
> Third: A daily striving for an **increased obedience** and perfection in our lives. Because of the perfect Atonement of Jesus, just men may be made perfect.
>
> Fourth: A **daily acknowledgment of His divinity**. To a daily, personal relationship with the Master, we must be His **disciples.**
>
> Fifth: A **daily study of the scriptures.** President Kimball has said: "I find that when I get casual in my relationships with divinity and when it seems that no divine ear is listening and no divine voice is speaking, that I am far, far away. If I immerse myself in the scriptures, the distance narrows and the spirituality returns."[2]

Those are just two examples. The 5 Star Day is timeless. I invite you to look for the 5 Star Day in the scriptures, words of modern-day prophets, and the life and ministry of the Savior. In doing so, you will confirm these wonderful truths as well as apply them more fully. It was by searching for these things in God's word that I was taught just how vital yet simple these daily actions are. These exhortations are not going to change. It is the Lord's 5 Star Day.

---

[2] James E. Faust, "A Personal Relationship with the Savior," *Ensign*, Nov. 1976, *lds.org*; The Church of Jesus Christ of Latter-day Saints, Nov. 1976 (accessed June 20, 2017); emphasis added; see also *Doctrine and Covenants* 76:69; Mosiah 5:13.

Where Do I Start?

Months ago I felt like I was physically dragging. I challenged my mom to do a "mile a day" challenge with me. Simply put, the goal was to run, or power walk, at least one mile a day for our exercise. We decided to do it around five times a week.

The first time we ran, we pretty much felt like blobs and we were panting like dogs. We stopped halfway and could not talk to each other. After catching our breath and stretching, we slowly started to run again. We finished the full mile, and it felt so good. It was very cleansing. High five and a "boo ya!"

After doing this consistently, we can now run more than a mile each day, we are getting faster, and we can have a conversation while doing it. We feel great each time we finish.

As we have done this challenge, my mom and I have noticed the parallel the "mile a day" has to a 5 Star Day. In relation to what running a mile is doing for our physical strength, we can feel that kind of renewal spiritually if we do certain things each day. If we regularly have a 5 Star Day, we will incrementally become "stronger and stronger" and "firmer and firmer" spiritually.[3]

If you feel spiritually "out of shape," just pick ONE of the Stars to work on for now. Remember, with time our mile challenge got easier. I testify that our "spiritual mile" will get easier for us as we are diligent. One thing that has been consistent during this mile challenge process is that we always feel good when we are done. It is spiritually symbolic that our choosing to run a mile a day feels good and has led to other healthy behaviors. Thus it is with the sincere, small efforts of a 5 Star Day. Start somewhere; it will undoubtedly cause a positive ripple effect.[4]

After starting simple, step-by-step strive to incorporate *all* the Stars; this is important. Remember what I taught in the beginning.

---

[3] Helaman 3:35.
[4] Robert D. Hales, "Becoming a Disciple of Our Lord Jesus Christ," *Ensign*, May 2017, 46-48.

Literally every single time I have felt spiritually off, far from God, apathetic, or discontent, I reanalyze my priorities and I come to find that there was a Star—or several Stars—consistently missing from my day-to-day life. Once I get back on track, the divine contentment returns.

With time, negligence of any Star has an effect on our overall happiness. We need all of them. And why wouldn't we want all of them? Greater peace, guidance, and simplicity…this is the reality! I think those are blessings we can all seek for, and I know they are blessings that the Lord is willing to give.[5]

The Long Term Effects

This analogy given by my dad sums up everything we have learned with the 5 Star Day. Pay attention to how you feel and what the Spirit teaches you. This spiritually symbolic experience can be applied to every one of us. My dad wrote:

On January 20th, 1984, Christine and I were married in the Jordan River Temple. A few months later we celebrated Christine's birthday. For her birthday I bought her a plant. Although not a very romantic gift, we needed some things to decorate our place…and I thought a plant would help. Remarkably, this plant is still alive today after almost 30 years!

WHY: Because Christine has taken care of the plant and watered and nourished it and allowed the sunlight to strengthen it. The plant is bigger and healthier today than ever before.

QUESTION: Even after all this time, what would happen if we placed the plant in a dark closet for a few weeks and ignored it? Most likely it'd die. Without sunlight and water the plant would slowly wither, and eventually perish.

ANALOGY: Our Testimony of the gospel of Jesus Christ is much like this plant. As we nourish our souls with "spiritual food" [a consistent 5 Star

---

[5] Alma 5:34; Jeremiah 29:13; Mosiah 7:33; *Doctrine and Covenants* 112:10; Matthew 11:28-30; see also Thomas S. Monson, "Consider the Blessings," *Ensign*, Nov. 2012, 86-89.

Day], our testimony will remain strong. If we place ourselves in the great and spacious building (Lehi's dream), or in a spiritually dark place, and stop nourishing our souls...then our testimony will slowly wither and weaken.[6] *Have you ever seen a person who was once very righteous and strong in the gospel, and then later in life they lost their way and testimony?*

How does this happen? Sometimes they place themselves in dark places by their actions and choices. Satan slowly and craftily wraps his chains around them and deceives them with the intent to drag them down to hell where they will be miserable forever like he is.[7] *Thankfully, the Atonement of Jesus Christ allows us all to repent of our mistakes and sins, and we can be forgiven. A very weak testimony can be nourished back to strength by consistency in the small things, humility, and obedience.*

May we always do those things that nourish our testimonies, and strengthen our souls: Pray often, study the scriptures daily, attend the temple regularly, attend church and partake of the sacrament each week, smile, and serve others. As we do these things, our testimony will remain strong, God will bless us, and we will be happy (even if we have trials in our lives). As Grandma Hansen always said, "When you are disobedient, you will always get hurt." [8]

I love these thoughts! I have seen weakened testimonies become strong once again, and firm testimonies remain strong through daily spiritual nourishment.

Remember the invitation at the beginning of this book to plant the 5 Star Day "seed" and give it time to "take root" and "grow" in your life? My sister, Ashton, noted that if we "neglect the tree, and take no thought for its nourishment" the 5 Star Day will not take root in our lives.[9] With "diligence...patience...and faith" the 5 Star Day will bring forth "fruit" and eternal benefits.[10] *Give it a try* and *stick with it.*

---

[6] 1 Nephi 8:26-28.
[7] 2 Nephi 28:21.
[8] Refer to Alma 41:10; Mosiah 2:41.
[9] Alma 32:38-40.
[10] Alma 32:41-43.

My Final Thoughts

My dear friend, I want to conclude this book with a few final thoughts before I send you off to resume your life's journey. Please Remember how valuable and capable you are! You matter to God. May you ever show Him that He matters to you. As my sister would say, "Through God's guidance you can know if you are exactly *where* you are supposed to be today. Now the key is to be *doing* exactly what you are supposed to be *doing* there today."

Please Remember the importance of **scripture study** daily. Get that armor on and steadfastly hold to the word of God! Remember that power comes from **sincere prayer**. Divine peace and direction from God can be a reality, and sincerity in our prayers is the key! Oh Remember to do something for someone daily through genuine **service**. Unselfish acts of kindness change lives! How greatly we need **sacred time** daily. In the midst of this busy world, may we choose to reconnect with heaven and Remember! Lastly, Remember to **smile** every single day of your life; gratitude and Christ's joy will illuminate your life and illuminate the other Stars!

I know that God is our loving Heavenly Father. I know this because I can feel His guidance in my life and His love when I pray. I know Jesus Christ really is the Savior of the world. I know this because I have felt His atoning power in my life. I am in the process of godly transformation, and it is all because of Him. I know that we have living prophets and apostles today. I have heard them speak, and as I prayerfully ponder their words I feel the Spirit testify to me that they are called of God. I know that Joseph Smith was called as the Lord's prophet to restore the fullness of Christ's gospel and church upon the earth. As I read of the miraculous experience that took place in the Sacred Grove, I cannot deny that I feel joy and a confirmation that these things are true. I also know that Joseph's divine call was real because I have read the Book of Mormon and prayed to God to know if it is true. I cannot deny the peace and joy that I feel as I read it. I know that the 5 Star Day can be a glorious tool in this life. It is the Lord's 5 Star Day. *These truly are five simple acts that change everything.* The Savior is the source of grace and truth.[11] May we choose to build our lives with Christ as our foundation! If we do this, we "cannot fall."[12] Please Remember that we want No Empty Chairs in the kingdom of God.

I love you, God loves you, and I know the things taught and testified of in this book will bring greater joy, peace, and eternal purpose to anyone who will consistently apply them. Let's get goin'!

Make It a 5 Star Day!

* **S**cripture Study—*Steadfastly hold to the word of God!*
* **S**incere Prayer—*Sincerity is the key!*
* **S**ervice—*Do something for someone every day!*
* **S**acred Time—*Reconnect and Remember.*
* **S**mile—*Be grateful and smile. Christ is joy.*

Testimonies

Janessa O. (Iowa City, IO)

When I started the second semester of the nursing program at BYU-Idaho, life went from busy to crazy busy. I was getting between four to five hours of sleep on average. I didn't even take the time to microwave my oatmeal or frozen peas; I ate things cold. I was in survival mode and was quickly burning out. I was so overwhelmed with how much I felt I needed to do each day. I remember sitting down and asking myself the question, "Janessa, what are the absolute essentials? What five things can I do each day that I would then consider my day a success?" This was the birth of the 5 Star Day. I wrote it on my little white board: "Make it a 5 Star Day" and listed the five things. They were: sincere

---

[11] John 1:17.
[12] Helaman 5:12.

prayer (morning, meals, and night), scripture study, serve someone, reach outside my comfort zone, and keep a daily journal.

Writing down and committing to these five small and simple gospel basics brought peace and clarity. *I was finally putting first things first.* And everything else fell into place. I felt the Lord's help managing the rest. I became a firm believer in the 5 Star Day. It takes conscientious effort and diligence, but the dividends are great. Kayla has since deepened and enhanced some of the Stars and renamed some in a way that is easier to remember, and those are the Stars I utilize today.

I compare the 5 Star Day to being physically fit. There are components such as: a well-balanced diet, cardio exercise, muscle strength, stretching/balance, and sleep/relaxation. All these work together to create optimal physical health. Our spirit is a living part of our being that also needs daily care, exercise, and nourishment. The 5 Star Day leads to optimal spiritual health.

Being spiritually fit includes these components: the word of God nourishes our spirits, heartfelt communication with God is central to our spiritual wellbeing, service adds substance to who we are (like strength training), striving to improve daily will stretch and balance our spirits, and pondering and gratitude in journal keeping brings clarity and perspective (like proper sleep).

When I neglect to do one, or more, of these essentials, I find that I am off-balance, or lacking strength spiritually. Prolonged neglect leads to spiritual malnutrition, atrophy, nearsightedness, and a hardened heart.

The Lord cares very much about the condition of our spiritual heart. He wants us to see clearly. He wants us to be strong like He is strong. He wants us to be filled with Truth. The 5 Star Day brings peace, direction, and joy to my life.

Eight years have passed. My circumstances have changed. I am now in the trenches of mothering many small children. Yet much remains the same. There is still way more to do in a day than I have time or energy to complete. I still need to put first things first. And I still need the Lord's help every single day. And I always will. The same Stars will apply and help me throughout the rest of my life.

Make It a 5 Star Day!

Taurie T. (Selah, WA)

The 5 Star Day helps me in every aspect of my life. When I am having a 5 Star Day, I notice many good things happen. I am happier, I am able to get more done throughout the day, and I feel closer to our Heavenly Father.

I have also found that when I have a 5 Star Day I am more aware of myself, and of others. I notice what I do well, what I can improve on, and I notice what those around me need. I also find that I am satisfied with myself, and with life, when I remember to do the little things in a 5 Star Day. Life just seems easier and more manageable when following the 5 Star Day. I am thankful for this pattern to help me to remember to do the little things every day. It truly is the little things that matter.

Jake H. (Idaho Falls, ID)

The 5 Star Day is a concept and a way of life that I wish everyone knew about. It is only through each aspect working together as a whole that we can truly maximize our happiness in this life, and grow closer to our Heavenly Father.

I have a testimony of these simple truths. I want to take a minute to talk about one Star in particular though. The Star Sacred Time Star is so important. We are all busy, and often we get caught up in school, work, church, family, and other affairs. While these are all necessary and wholesome things, the daily choice to review and reflect on our lives is absolutely vital. The Spirit speaks by a still, small voice. If we are looking for answers to our prayers or for solutions to problems in our lives, how will we ever get those answers if we don't give the Spirit a chance to speak to us?

Personally, I find myself most in tune with the spirit through music. Each day, I sit at the piano and play through songs I have written over the years. As I sit and listen, forgetting about my homework assignment due the next morning, I feel a sense of peace that is so healing. While we may all be busy, if we take just a moment each day to reflect on our life, and listen to the Holy Ghost, we will feel a sense of contentment that is so unnatural in today's upbeat, crazy world.

Anna S. (Denver, CO)

One of my favorite parts of a 5 Star day is Smile. I am a person who smiles and laughs a lot throughout the day. I am also a person who suffers from depression nearly every day in some form. There was a period in my life where I would think multiple times a day about taking my own life. Sometimes on those days it was hard to smile, but I had others around me that helped me smile.

For those who are reading this I would like to encourage you to Smile on a daily basis, truly smile because you never know who will need your smile. During those rough days when you find it hard to smile, be true to yourself and allow others—and the Lord—to help you Smile.

The 5 Star Day as a whole is essential. Elder L Whitney Clayton taught:

> *The trial of our faith will always involve staying true to simple, daily practices of faith. Then, and only then, does He promise that we will receive the divine response for which we long. Only once we have proven our willingness to do what He asks without demanding to know the whens, the whys, and the hows do we "reap the rewards of [our] faith, and [our] diligence, and patience, and long-suffering.." Real obedience accepts God's commandments unconditionally and in advance.*[13]

Jacoby R. (Modesto, CA) (Email sent while serving in Ecuador)

At Zone conference today we focused a lot on the basics like service, scripture study, and prayer and that reminded me of some great advice that my cousin Kayla gave me a while ago. Kayla encouraged 5 basic things to do every day in order to make every day a 5 Star Day.

Haha yes I know it's cheesy, but I'm telling you these bad boys really do work! Try it if you don't believe me, and I promise you'll be happier and your life will be more fulfilling and have greater purpose. The Lord's work is moving forward, and I'm grateful to be a part of this marvelous work and a wonder!

---

[13] L. Whitney Clayton, "Whatsoever He Saith unto You, Do It," *Ensign*, May 2017, 97-99; see also Alma 32:43.

Make It a 5 Star Day!

The Church of Jesus Christ of Latter-day Saints is true, and it is the only place where we can find complete peace in this life, and eternal salvation in the life to come.

Darlene S. (Lindon, UT)

I love the 5 Star Day concept because they are so basic and simple (doable), yet so profound if we do them. I find that the days go by so quickly. Before I know it, it's time for bed. Sometimes at the end of the day, it seems like the day has just begun! I often ask myself where did the time go, and why didn't I get everything done I wanted to?

If I start my day with scripture study and sincere prayer, my day always goes better. I feel like I am ahead. If I get distracted, I feel like I am trying to catch up all day because it weighs on my shoulders, and it feels like I always have one more thing to do until it gets done.

There are storms all around us today. There are a lot of things that are out of our control, and we need to learn to smile and be glad for our lives and for the blessings we do have. Heavenly Father knows what is best for us to learn and to grow. I know if we can look at our trials as being "FOR" us instead of "TO" us, we can have eternal perspective on everything.

I love Ether 2:24-25. In this passage, the Lord is telling the brother of Jared what they can expect on their journey to the promised land. The Lord talks about the "mountain waves shall dash upon them," and they will be "like a whale in the ocean." God says He will "bring them up from the depths of the sea" and the "winds and the rains and floods He will send forth out of His mouth." It shows that Heavenly Father is mighty to be able to save us if we turn to Him. He will lift us out of the depths (sorrows, sins, discouragement, despair, depression, etc.) whatever "depths" we are buried in. I don't believe God sends us every trial in our lives, but I do know that He lets some things happen for our growth to get us to where He wants us to be spiritually. I especially love in verse 25 how the Lord says: "I prepare you against these things, for ye cannot cross

212

this great deep save I prepare you."[14] *We can be grateful that He has given us some amazing gifts that help to prepare our way.*

A 5 Star Day puts all those gifts into perspective! Thank goodness Heavenly Father expects us to just keep trying!

Ashton H. (Mountain View, CA)

THE 5 STAR DAY! In today's world we can choose to experience certain things that can have a rating of 5 Stars. Some examples are: restaurants, hotels, movies, books, etc. Some words that would describe something that has a rating of 5 STARS would be: amazing, fantastic, marvelous, wonderful, top-notch, magnificent. Having a 5 Star experience is one that you will not easily forget! It is also an experience that comes with a cost. Often the amount that we put into something, or pay for something, yields the quality. If someone told you that you could have a DAY that is magnificent, meaningful, marvelous, amazing, wonderful…would you not want a 5 Star Day?!

<u>*I am telling you, from consistent application of this in my life, it is worth it. It really does work.*</u> *Whenever I am having a less than excellent day, I take a look at the 5 Stars and can often immediately recognize the missing ones. As I then go and do them, my day most assuredly improves. This 5 Star Day formula is the framework to my daily habits that help me to stay connected to God, self, and others. This formula has changed my life.*

The consistent application of it has brought me added peace, purpose, joy, and better awareness of my self-worth. As I live the 5 Star Day, I can tangibly feel a greater measure of the Spirit in my life which helps guide me to be an instrument in the Lord's hands. This, in turn, allows me to emulate more Christ-like attributes in my interactions with others.

I appreciate having the simple 5 Star Formula to help me REMEMBER the importance of nourishing my soul each day. It is easy to remember and has become a part of me, not just something to check off each day. I feel that I have truly planted the 5 Star Day seed into my life, and I am now tasting the fruits. They are oh so sweet, and worth it.

---

[14] Ether 2:25.

About the Author

Kayla Hansen is a fun-loving daughter of God with a passion for the gospel of Jesus Christ. God and her family are her two greatest sources of joy. She is thankful for the goodness that her friends and family have brought into her life.

She is especially grateful for the Lord and His teachings. After years of research and gospel study, she wrote this book under the direction of the Spirit. The 5 Star Day has everything to do with the Savior. This is her first book, but it may not be her last.

She graduated from Brigham Young University-Idaho with her Bachelor's degree in Nursing. Her experience working as a nurse has included: pediatrics, geriatrics, stroke and trauma rehab, and mental health. She has appreciated her coworkers throughout the years, and she loves her patients.

Kayla served as a full-time proselyting missionary in Neuquén, Argentina. In addition to preaching Jesus Christ's gospel, she served faithfully in her primary assignment as the mission nurse. She loves Argentina and everyone she served with.

She also enjoys dancing, writing songs on her ukulele, speaking Spanish, making new friends, traveling, playing sports, jogging, and eating lots of oatmeal.

Made in the USA
Columbia, SC
18 July 2022